*Examination Copy*

ROMANTICISM AND REVOLT

*W*e are pleased to send you
this book, with our compliments,
so that you may have an
opportunity to review it for
possible class use. We hope you
will enjoy examining it.

Price $2.95

Harcourt, Brace & World, Inc.

757 Third Avenue, New York, New York 10017
7555 Caldwell Avenue, Chicago, Illinois 60648
Polk and Geary, San Francisco, California 94109
1372 Peachtree Street, N.E., Atlanta, Georgia 30309

# ROMANTICISM AND REVOLT

## EUROPE 1815–1848

### J. L. TALMON

HARCOURT, BRACE & WORLD, INC.

First American Edition 1967

REPRINTED 1968

Library of Congress Catalog Card Number: 67-22480

PRINTED IN GREAT BRITAIN BY JARROLD AND SONS LTD NORWICH

# CONTENTS

FOREWORD                                                    7

I INTRODUCTION                                             9

The theme                                                  9
Being and becoming                                        12
*The international order*                                  14
*Social foundations and changed self-awareness*           16

II THE GRAND DEBATE                                       21

Social mobility                                           21
The divine order and the sovereign self-sufficient state  23
Authority versus liberty                                  29
The politics of plot and riot                             32
The split                                                 39
Property                                                  42

III SOCIALISM                                             51

Origins                                                   51
Romantic technocracy                                      58
Utopia                                                    68
Ferment in France                                         72
The British way                                           76
The German ingredient from Kant to Marx                  81
*Philosophical preparation*                               82
*The young Marx*                                          90

IV NATIONALISM                                      95

   Sources of inspiration                           95
   Idée force                                      101
   Identity and diversity                          106
   Greece                                          110
   Italy                                           115
   Germany                                         121

V ROMANTICISM                                      135

   A spirit astir                                  135
   The I                                           136
   The Universe                                    150
   'Prometheus Unbound'                             157
   'A light, a glory . . .'                        162

VI 1848: THE YEAR OF TRIAL                         166

   A spectre becomes flesh                         166
   From general concord to class war: France       170
   Conflict of nations: Mitteleuropa               174
   Realism triumphant                              188

STATISTICS                                         197

BIBLIOGRAPHY                                       200

LIST OF ILLUSTRATIONS                              208

INDEX                                              212

A book should speak so clearly for itself that there should be no need for a Foreword to explain the author's intentions or to apologize for his failures. Yet so great is the fear of being misunderstood and so intense the anxiety to forestall criticism for not having done what one had not thought of doing that few authors can resist the temptation.

It is not my intention to offer a record of what went on in the various European countries during the years 1815–48. My aim is to delineate those forces and trends which were at work everywhere, and whose interaction gave a distinct character and a unity to the age. Too general history is bad history. I have therefore tried to make the reader aware of the local and national versions of the universal currents. The beam of the projector is not focused on the leading nations as such, but is kept shifting from one significant development to another. These have been selected for their pioneering nature, their character as typical samples or test cases, the effectiveness of their impact, or their focal role in the context of conflict and clash.

There are few periods in history which bring into relief so strikingly as the years between 1815 and 1848 the fact that each period is no more than a station in the historical process. During the age of Romanticism and revolt the trauma of the French Revolution worked itself out in the texture of the developments stimulated by the Industrial Revolution, though the solutions formulated by contemporaries were put to the test at a later period and were realized, if at all, in a manner very different from the one originally envisaged. If the interaction of the old and the new, the permanent and the contingent, be our concern, still more so is the complex relationship (and by no means the simple and direct 'being and consciousness' model) between the nature of things and the image men formed thereof out of their divergent interests, convictions and wishes, and not least, as we have only too painfully learned in our own time, out of their traumatic experiences and obsessive memories – the source of so much conflict and frustration.

My natural penchant has led me to dwell more on patterns of mind and behaviour than on the substratum of social-economic realities. I have done this partly because of my reluctance simply to copy or paraphrase what others have already done on the basis of first-hand knowledge and with a competence much greater than I could aspire to. I am also convinced that the recent tendency to turn history into statistical survey and sociological analysis – one might call it social geology – has gone far enough, and that it is time for a corrective in the direction of human drama. All the same, the subject of this book may be considered as both geology and drama. All the problems, ideas and conflicts of the modern age are already there in *statu nascendi*. And few would deny that if 1789 released vast discordant forces, these reached a tragic denouement in the years 1848–9 – a drama with an almost classical unity.

I wish to acknowledge with thanks the help I received from Drs Shlomo Avineri and Israel Kolatt, Miss Zohar Ariel, Miss P. Weiss, Mr Michael Heyd, and Mrs Efrath B. Kleinhaus who compiled the Index. My special thanks go to Mr Stanley Baron for the care he took in polishing my English.

'There is only one serious matter in Europe in 1832', Metternich wrote, 'and that is revolution' – by which he meant not palace or political revolution 'but social revolution [which] attacks the foundations of society'. In the same year, the British Ambassador in Vienna, Sir Frederick Lamb, expressed the opinion that 'the principle of movement and that of repose are at war openly or underhand throughout Europe, and people are much more liberal or the reverse than they are Frenchmen, or Germans, or Italians'.

The spokesman of Holy Alliance universalism and the representative of insular Britain both seemed to agree that the fate of Europe was being shaped not so much by what was going on within the frontiers of the existing states, in accordance with each country's particular situation and tradition, or by the rivalries among them as sovereign powers, as by a single common force at work everywhere. And yet – an apparent contradiction – this was the age of the rise of nationalism, seemingly the least universal of all creeds. The truth is that although in each case the modalities of nationalism differed as a result of a particular geo-political situation, history and social structure, nationalists of all lands felt themselves united in a common struggle against dynastic legitimism. Up to the hour of trial – 1848 – it is reasonable to speak of a peoples' camp facing an alliance of kings.

The single propelling force of the age was, to use modern terminology, the trauma of revolution. A man of Metternich's cast of mind could find no other explanation for that restless drive for revolutionary change than a sudden swelling of human rebelliousness – the rejection of the principle of authority, first divine and then social-political. An Englishman, the Romantic poet Southey, revolutionary turned arch-Tory, was able to see deeper: 'the steam

9

engine and the spinning engines, the mail coach and the free publication of the debates in parliament. . . . Hence follow in natural and necessary consequences increased activity, enterprise, wealth and power; but on the other hand, greediness of gain, looseness of principle, wretchedness, disaffection and political insecurity.'

It was the coalescence of two vast Revolutions, the French and the Industrial, that determined both the shape of things and the frame of mind of the age up to 1848. The historian is in many cases at a loss to decide which was more effective – reality or image – since the latter had all the compulsive intensity of an obsession which perhaps proved no less potent than coal and iron, armaments and statistics.

The French Revolution and Napoleon brought about enormous objective changes in every field. Furthermore, the very possibility of such a vast and sudden transformation was an extraordinary and shattering idea to men accustomed to a static traditional existence. But there was more to it than the shock of an isolated and closed catastrophic event even if it seemed to suggest that other such

occurrences might take place at any time. There was no one, Right, Left or Centre, who was not convinced that the forces released by the two Revolutions – the French and the Industrial – were driving the world irresistibly onwards upon a course of tremendous changes. Some felt the exalting hope that the wagon of history was being precipitated to a preordained, final station where scientific rationality and social justice would replace irrational tradition, wasteful pain-inflicting drift and selfish avarice. Others were possessed by an apocalyptic dread of chaos and horror. Then there were those who with mixed feelings endeavoured to tame the violent forces which had been unleashed.

The social-economic changes resulting from technological developments proceeded inexorably, without regard to ideological presuppositions, expectations or fears. But this is only a half-truth. The impact of these changes was largely conditioned by the significance men were disposed to attach to them as a result of their preoccupation with the French Revolution and its repercussions. And nothing proves this more convincingly than – again – the rise of nationalism.

1   Cartoon of 1821 showing confusion and anarchy in an English revolutionary association

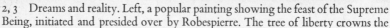

2, 3 Dreams and reality. Left, a popular painting showing the feast of the Supreme
Being, initiated and presided over by Robespierre. The tree of liberty crowns the

For however much its fortunes might in each particular case be
determined by social-economic circumstances, it could by no means
be regarded as merely an outcome of them.

## BEING AND BECOMING

Revolution (abortive) and Romanticism – the two salient features
of the age – are to a large extent explained by the fact that expectations, intensified by a traumatic experience of break with the past,
by far outran the realities of objective change. Hence the proneness
of the disappointed to revolt and the romantic quest of the bewildered for personal and collective identity; hence too the tremendous endeavours of philosophers and Utopian dreamers to offer
a total and foolproof explanation of social, not to say cosmic, reality,
combining diversity with unity, change with continuity.

No wonder that the leading philosopher of the age, Hegel, was
so fascinated by the problem of being and becoming. The historian

hill-top. Right, one of the triumphs of English technology: the opening of the Canterbury–Whitstable Railway

indeed is bound to ask himself which is his task: to offer a photographic record by concentrating on those events and activities which loomed largest in their own time; or to focus his sights on things often still quantitatively insignificant but potentially highly effective, and destined to become dominant. The millions of history-less peasants plodding on, 'who spoke not, but were France'? or the contrivances of isolated mechanics, the rattling of a few hundred engines and the puffing of some scores of tall chimneys? The set sermons of thousands of parish priests to millions of worshippers? or the incantations of obscure scribes and the agitation of tiny groups of their exalted followers?

In this book the second course has been followed. It is not concerned with photographic likeness but with distillation of significance; not with these few decades as a closed period, but with a juncture in humanity's march from the past to the future; in brief, not so much with being as with becoming.

1815–48: the age of revolt and change. Yet when compared with 1815, the map of Europe in 1848 (and for that matter, of 1850, after the failure of the 1848 revolutions) shows only two comparatively slight changes: the Kingdom of the Netherlands set up in 1815 had in 1830 split into Holland and Belgium; and, at about the same time, an independent Greek state had been carved out of the southern tip of the Balkan peninsula, almost the whole of which remained under the shaky suzerainty of the Sultans. The pedant might insist on another change: in 1846 Austria, with the blessing of her two partners in the murder of Poland, absorbed the Cracow region, which had been proclaimed a free Polish city in 1815. The last (symbolic) vestige of an independent Polish nation was thereby effaced.

There were six great powers in Europe in the period between 1815 and 1848. Of these, two were constitutional monarchies and nation states – France and England; three were absolute multi-national empires – Russia, Austria and tottering Turkey; and one was a dynastic state – Prussia. There were two territorial patchworks eager to be united – the German Confederation of over thirty units and the Italian peninsula, with over half a dozen states, most of them under foreign dynasties. The Iberian nations had given up all initiative long before they lost their American empires, and their constant internal troubles were a standing invitation to foreign intervention and rivalry. Scandinavia made its political presence felt chiefly through the vexed Schleswig-Holstein dispute between Denmark and Germany.

The sole serious disturbances of international peace occurred on the periphery of Europe – the war between Russia and Turkey around 1830 and the Mehemet Ali imbroglio some years later. The latter shook the decrepit Ottoman Empire to its foundations and brought the rivalries between the great powers to crisis-point; yet, like the earlier incident, it was solved without a general war. In the wider world, the period seems like a lull between the colonial wars of the eighteenth century and the imperialist scramble of the last quarter of the nineteenth. The North Americans continued their

4   Map of the European frontiers in 1815

drive westward, bringing under the plough vast stretches of land, and enlarging the number of the states of the Union. South of it, and under its inspiration, a whole continent shook off the feeble rule of Spain and Portugal and split into a score or so of independent states. After inheriting from Holland the Cape and Ceylon, Britain succeeded in further consolidating its possessions in India and the Malayan peninsula.

Russia was systematically extending her sway into the Caucasus, Central Asia and Eastern Siberia. China, like Japan, still stood aside from the main currents of events, almost hermetically sealed off, except for one occurrence. The forced opening of five ports to European trade at the end of the Opium War between China and Britain impressed contemporaries little, but looms large a century later. While Canada, Australia and New Zealand were gradually evolving from colony to Dominion, the Black Continent continued

5, 6  Two views of the Vienna Congress. Below, the ludicrous antics of the crowned heads and nobles assembled in 1815 to redraw the map of Europe; right, a group portrait of the negotiators by Isabey

LE CONGRÈS.

to be, except for the Portuguese and some other marginal areas, a *terra incognita*. Only on the two extremities of the African continent did changes take place which bore seeds of grave complications in the distant future: France annexed Algeria, and the Boers in South Africa set out on their trek to escape British rule but were then again brought under imperial government in the new state of Natal.

Paradoxically, the age of Romanticism and revolt experienced only one change of régime through revolution: the 1830 July Revolution in France. Innumerable plots, conspiracies, *coups, journées* and revolts failed, notwithstanding the vast ferment of revolutionary liberal, democratic and socialist ideas. Nationalist fervour held in grip the noblest minds and hearts of the youth of subjugated or divided nations. Yet only the small Belgian and Greek nationalities succeeded in gaining their liberty.

*Social foundations and changed self-awareness*

The political foundations of the official order of the age were laid by the monarchs and titled grandees round the Vienna Congress

table. Throughout the period, except perhaps in France under the July Monarchy, the fate of nations was seemingly still being decided by aristocrats of ancient lineage in splendid châteaux and country-houses over weekend and hunting parties – not in consultative assemblies, or in party caucuses in solid bourgeois drawing-rooms, or over the business counters of the great captains of industry and heads of banking interests; and still less in the tumultuous mass rallies of the common people or the secret conventicles of tense conspirators.

The liveried servants attending the well-born were still far more numerous than the industrial workers in pits, furnaces and cotton mills. And to the end of the period, with the exception of England, many more people continued to live in village cottages than were to be found crowded in large city slums, notwithstanding the constant migration of the rural proletariat, driven out by enclosure, in England, and elsewhere by agricultural reform and changed modes of agricultural production and notwithstanding the general population surplus.

The remarkable growth of population was indeed the most tangible symptom of change. It was as yet, however, a condition for the Industrial Revolution, in that it created the necessary man-power and increased the number of consumers; it was not a result of industrialism, though it was later to become so.

The railway was the only technological advance, and cotton the only industrial product, which significantly affected the way most men lived. The rapid growth of coal and iron production had little immediate effect on conditions of life, but was rather a function of railway and machine construction. New methods for producing steel had not yet been discovered and men had hardly learned to make use of the chemical by-products of minerals; in a country like France coke still had to face the competition of timber as smelting fuel.

Lighting and heating methods continued as of old. Refrigeration and the preservation of foodstuffs still belonged to the future. The steam-boat and railway had not yet become the vehicles for the rapid and ceaseless transportation of grain, foods, raw materials and industrial commodities from one corner of the earth to the other.

7 The Industrial Revolution in Germany: an iron-foundry in Neustadt-Eberswalde

8   The Industrial Revolution in Britain: a coal-mine in Yorkshire

Since space had not yet been really overcome, the succession of seasons and the benevolence of nature were still of vital importance. The threat of famine was still real: witness the disastrous years on the eve of 1848. With the possible exception of England, the crises of the age were more the result of bad harvests than of disturbances in the market mechanism. Nor had the threat of epidemics yet been ended: cholera spread across Europe and America in the early 1830s, and there were sporadic outbreaks of typhus and other scourges. The continental countries were only slowly and almost reluctantly learning the lessons of the early English agricultural revolution in tillage, drainage, irrigation, rotation of crops, rootcrops and stock-breeding. The old three-field system died hard. Conservatism, fear of hunger and a primitive sense of justice encouraged retention of the antiquated ways of smallholders, and militated against the improvements which only large-scale capitalist methods of production could secure – above all the enclosing of commons. Agricultural machines, which in America were the result of shortage of labour and the vastness of holdings, had hardly as yet reached Europe. Nor did chemical fertilizers play any significant part. In France and elsewhere bread

19

was still the mainstay of the diet of the poor, with the potato coming into its own in central and eastern Europe, and of course in Ireland.

One could summarize the Industrial Revolution up to 1848 as hardly more than a preparation of tools and capital goods for the real thing, with the sinews of expanding international capitalism – modern banking, joint stock shareholding, exchange and credit facilities – still, in spite of the Rothschilds and other bankers (the 'Kings' of the July Monarchy) only at an early take-off stage.

Yet the age was fascinated by and obsessively interested in the problems of industry. In the minds of the enlightened, political economy had now taken the place occupied by physics a century earlier. In particular, no topic was more discussed in the 1830s and 1840s than the social question. This was centred on the industrial workers in the new urban agglomerations which had grown at a fantastic speed – Manchester and Bradford, Roubaix and Saint-Étienne, the towns of Brabant, the Ruhr, Saxony and Silesia. Their miserable existence and long hours; child labour, disease, unemployment, insecurity and general degradation; the desperate struggle of spinners and weavers to compete with the machine – such things loomed much larger than was warranted by the numerical proportion of proletarians to the population as a whole. They did so because men were intensely conscious of a vast transformation afoot, and because the evils of industrialism contradicted so flagrantly the expectations and claims engendered by that transformation.

The sense of all-pervading structural crisis was thus not so much the inevitable outcome of a ripe industrial revolution as the reflection of a general revolutionary experience. The dislocation was disturbing because of its novelty and the unpreparedness of men, who had not yet learned how to deal with the new problems. Because of the traumatic memories which conditioned men's vision, it seemed to presage a catastrophic breakdown and denouement.

In brief, the general fabric of existence was not yet substantially different on the eve of 1848 from what it had been half a century earlier; but the whole framework was profoundly undermined by a totally changed self-awareness in men.

# II THE GRAND DEBATE

The two most far-reaching and permanent ideological and institutional legacies left by the French Revolution were the undisputed sovereignty as well as self-sufficiency of the state as a secular institution (versus the claims of religion), and the victory of the conception of a society based upon contract over the tradition of a society founded upon status: as John Stuart Mill put it in the essay on *The Subjection of Women* in an effort to define 'the most distinct feature' of 'modern life' – that 'human beings are no longer born to their place in life . . . but are free to employ their faculties . . . to achieve the lot which may appear to them most desirable.' The self-sufficiency of secular society and social mobility are indeed closely interconnected.

To take social mobility first. With the exception of Tsarist Russia and the Ottoman Empire, the individual on the European continent was in 1815, or was felt to be, on the way to becoming emancipated from any deterministic limitations set by birth. Personal serfdom had been abolished in France on the night of 4 August 1789. It was ended in most of the Italian and German states when they came under the control of Napoleon and under the influence of his Code, and in Prussia by the reforms initiated by Stein in 1807; in the Austrian domains, on the other hand, emancipation from 'robot' had to wait till 1848. Equality before the law was not affected in principle by the fact that, unlike those in France, the peasants in Prussia and elsewhere had to redeem their land in money or in kind by ceding a part of their holdings to the landlord; nor by certain local juridical and police powers left to the nobility over the peasants; nor by the survival of game laws and the hunting monopoly of the squires in England. This was more than offset by the laws which turned land into a commodity like any other, and abolished the prohibition of

21

9, 10  Post-Revolutionary cartoons contrasting 'The Frenchman of the past', 'nibbled at from all sides' (left), and 'The Frenchman of today', his motto 'Death to rats' (right)

land sale and land purchase between the various classes. To this must be added the dissolution of the guild system. This again occurred first in France, where ideological reasons received greater stress, then gradually, haltingly and partially in other states, where pressing needs were more decisive. Revolutionary France regarded any corporation as a restriction of the freedom of the individual, and also as the expression of a partial interest militating against the general good. The reform movement in Prussia was precipitated directly by the Jena catastrophe, and indirectly by the economic inefficiency of serfdom and the need to create a citizenship with a direct stake in the state. Man was, in theory at least, made free to choose his occupation, move about freely in pursuit of gain, sell his labour and his goods to anyone, and buy such commodities from whomever he chose – in brief, to make whatever he could of himself by his skill and good fortune. Everywhere objective developments and ideological trends combined to pave the way to individualism and social mobility. Serf labour had proved uneconomical, to some extent at least, because rumours about the rights of man had reached even illiterate peasants, and made them slack and unwilling to exert themselves. Steam and machines, which could well be served by totally unskilled labour, were making nonsense of the stern apprenticeship regulations. The laws regulating the size, type and quality of products and rules limiting competition and forestalling were about to be swept away by mass production and wide markets, with all the fluctuations of demand and supply which accompanied them. Even where corporations lingered on because of the continued preponderance of handicraft or conservative sentiment, no one doubted that these institutions were doomed. The same applies on a somewhat different plane to whatever was left in some places of entail and mainmorte. Needless to add it was only in England that social mobility assumed dimensions corresponding to the revolutionary nature of the principle. Yet class distinctions in England remained as rigid and the political repercussions so much less violent than elsewhere.

## THE DIVINE ORDER AND THE SOVEREIGN SELF-SUFFICIENT STATE

The vision (or spectre) of the free, mobile individual thrilled some and filled others with dread. The attitude of the former was a blend of hope of gain and faith in the goodness, power and perfectibility of men. That of the latter was a mixture of fear of losing existing advantages and a deep suspicion of man. Under the impact of the French Revolution, however, the dialogue was pursued upon the plane of absolutes. For the French Revolution had given birth to modern ideologies, indeed ideologies *tout court*; and ideologies fight shy of simple self-interest.

The men of 1789 appealed to universal and eternal principles because law, precedent and custom supported the established order. When custom and precedent were made to give way to natural laws, the upholders of the old system were driven to meet the revolutionaries on their own ground, that of general theory. Social mobility implied that there was no pre-existent order, that every order had been created by men as they saw fit and useful, by way of contrivance and contract. This meant that just as there was no divinely ordained social-economic order, there could be no political system claiming absolute legitimacy prior to the wills of men. The

23

progressives believed in the essentially social nature of men, while the less starry-eyed liberals put their trust in the benevolence of nature to reconcile individual egoisms in a pattern of social harmony and a free and stable political order.

The opposite attitude may be illustrated by Ludwig von Gerlach, the high priest of Prussian conservatism, who as late as 1864 took Bismarck to task for having forsaken and betrayed the sacred cause of combating the French Revolution – to Gerlach the supreme and ultimately sole test. The rising statesman had put patriotic egoism above God's command: he had dared to depose ancient dynasties, and in getting the Landtag to sanction retroactively the budgets which it had only a few years earlier refused to approve, he had by implication recognized popular sovereignty. Bismarck had thus raised a sacrilegious hand against the eternal, pre-existent divine order, and set a terrible example. The greater the fear of change resulting from social mobility, the greater was the need to uphold the value of traditional institutions, to subordinate the individual to the group and to anchor both to some eternal and objective scheme of things.

The progressives of all hues spoke of the rights of man: the reactionaries countered with the malignant fickleness of man and the omnipotent, benevolent wisdom of God. This is why the extreme protagonists – de Maistre, Bonald and Ludwig von Haller on the one side, Karl Marx and Blanqui on the other – never tired of repeating that the religious issue was the linchpin of the social order. De Maistre writes *Du Pape*, advocating the restoration of the papacy to the position of supreme arbiter among nations; Feuerbach sets out to prove that it was not God who had created man, but man who had created God in order to explain and justify his own misery; and David Friedrich Strauss denies that Jesus Christ ever existed.

Only a few theocrats like the young Lamennais could be consistent to the end. The position of the reactionaries was undermined by having confronted the Rationalist revolutionary ideology with an appeal to history and national tradition. For the uniqueness of a national personality did not go very well with theocratic, papal universalism. The reactionaries were not unaware of the difficulty, and tried to meet it by pointing out that the religious tradition was an essential ingredient in the evolution of every historic national personality in Europe. What would French history be without Catholicism? This argument played into the hands of the liberals, since it could be taken to suggest that religion was a pragmatic device unconsciously chosen by the nation in its struggle for existence. Thus Gallicanism was bitterly fought by some Ultramontanes as likely to lead to the liberal conception of a self-sufficient national state established by men deliberating together and signing a social contract.

If Gallicanism was intellectually untenable, consistent Ultramontanism was impossible. However much in need of the religious prop, even the most reactionary government could not agree to subordinate national sovereignty to papal supremacy, notwithstanding all the logic of de Maistre, the passion of Lamennais, and the visionary nostalgia of Novalis. The French Revolution, not to speak of the instinctive nationalism of the old monarchies, had made that impossible. The state could no longer be made into a part of the Christian universal order. The Church had by then become only one of the societies within the framework of the nation state. It is no accident that while concordats were concluded between Rome and most of the states on the morrow of 1815, Austria and Spain, the two most Catholic monarchies, were the exception. In those states there was, as it were, no need to regulate relations and delimit respective rights and powers. No less ironical was of course the fact that the Holy Alliance was signed by one ruler who was a schismatic (Alexander of Russia), another a Protestant heretic (Frederick William III of Prussia), and a third, His Apostolic Majesty Francis I of Austria, who became a party to the arrangement in the teeth of an explicit papal condemnation. Paradoxically, the Vicar of Christ would have nothing to do with the endeavour to enthrone Christian principles in international politics.

In the Protestant parts of Germany the situation was in this respect more complicated. Although the Lutheran Church was traditionally subordinated to the state, the Ultramontanes preached that the French Revolution was really started by that arch-rebel

Martin Luther. A number of Protestant romantics indeed ended as Roman Catholics or came near to embracing Catholicism, and it was after all the youthful Protestant Novalis who was one of the first, if not the very first, to sing the glories of a united Christian Europe under the aegis of the papacy. All the same, the exigencies of the sovereign and self-sufficient state forced a deeply religious king of Prussia to arrest a Catholic archbishop whose stand on mixed marriages threatened the unity of the nation and the sovereignty of the state. Many conservative Protestants were deeply chagrined by this, just as a generation later ultra-conservative Protestants in Germany objected to Bismarck playing into the hands of godless liberalism by harassing Catholic priests.

Protestant and Catholic conservatives in Germany shared a detestation and fear of *laissez-faire* economic liberalism. 'Manchesterism' was to them the manifestation of utter selfishness, on a par with the self-willed rebelliousness of the French revolutionary tradition. Hence their hankering for guilds and corporations, and indeed protectionism.

The conservatives in France were unable to sustain the half-hearted efforts which had been made to subordinate education to ecclesiastical control by putting a bishop at the head of the University or abolishing the monopoly of the University. The support given to the officially banned Orders, the policy of associating all national manifestations with religious rites and solemnities, the official encouragement given to feasts and rallies of expiation (a religious replica of the Revolutionary *fêtes de la fédération*, with planting of crosses instead of liberty trees), and finally the laws against sacrilege and blasphemy – all had the effect of making the government look ridiculous rather than fearful. These efforts appeared to be almost an attack on the national spirit of France, while their repressive aspects were seen as a dire threat to freedom of self-expression, especially the liberty of the press. The religious question rather than the one milliard indemnity to the émigrés became the burning issue. Nationalism and liberalism were united by and against the alliance of altar and throne, and in conjunction brought down the Restoration monarchy in 1830.

11, 12 An allegorical painting of 1802 (left) celebrates Napoleon's re-establishment of religion in France through the Concordat of the same year. Right: popular painting of a *fête de la fédération*, 1790

In England the situation was different. The Anglican establishment remained the rock of the Tory tradition, second only to the monarchy; but the Tories had long before ceased to be Jacobites. Even those Tories who considered parliamentary institutions a danger to the Continental monarchies were not prepared to see England ruled by an absolute king without parliament – though, of course, they opposed parliamentary reform. Burke himself never preached a return to divine-right absolutism or the establishment of a theocracy. He only decried the absurd presumption that a body politic could be artificially contrived by pure reason, with the aid of a few abstract syllogisms. To Burke the divine order was the British constitution, and he tried anxiously to discover also the mighty, many-branched tree of the constitution of ancient France. The Continental followers of the author of *Reflections on the French Revolution*, Gentz, Haller, Adam Müller, Bonald, were altogether more

27

metaphysical and, having no such constitution to lean upon, were compelled to give a theocratic twist to Burke.

A nation which owed its glory to free institutions and its power to world-wide trade was not likely to lend much attention to the kind of Romanticism which Disraeli's 'Young England' movement tried to spread in England. Aristocrats continued in practice to preside over the destinies of England; but the ideal of a natural aristocratic leadership, protecting the mass of the common people against the moneyed classes, fell on deaf ears. And industrial expansion and conquering capitalism could not be stopped by eloquent jeremiads about the soulless machine and the depersonalization of human relationships.

High Toryism may have had visions of the pre-existence of an objective establishment based on the indivisible Anglican Church (in spite of Catholic emancipation and the 'arrival' of the Dissenters) and of the preponderance of landed property – in short, of an order into which men are born – but the Protestant tradition, economic interests and the parliamentary régime rendered these ideas wholly ineffective. There being no powerful provocation, the English forces of movement and change never developed anti-religious attitudes. If nineteenth-century England was saved from a revolution by

14   In England, religion [i]s a factor in the main[ten]ance of stability. Left, [ev]ening prayers as a domestic [dis]cipline in a country-house; [rig]ht, an engraving by Doré [of] a Bible-reader in a night [ref]uge

religion, as has been suggested, it was not a religion imposed and backed by the Establishment, but a religious wave coming from below. Moreover, Methodism and the Evangelical movement helped conservatism in other ways than just by emphasizing discipline in personal conduct and dwelling upon the unimportance of the things of this world. They also offered an outlet – elsewhere provided by the politics of conspiracy and riot – to the craving for self-expression, and a framework for the need of men to associate in wider fellowships or closely-knit small groups.

AUTHORITY VERSUS LIBERTY

The problem of authority versus liberty, organic tradition versus social mobility and individualism, dominated political life in western Europe until 1830, and that of eastern Europe until 1848. It was at bottom an argument about the source of sovereignty and legitimacy. Louis XVIII of France was able to ask somebody congratulating him on having at last become king, 'Have I ever ceased to be king?' and to refuse to acknowledge the fact that he was called to the throne in 1814 by the Imperial Senate, a body representative of the nation though not really elected by it. The Charter was not a constitution embodying the social contract but a concession granted by the king

29

to the nation. Charles X was stating something quite obvious to him and, as he thought, to everyone else, when he said that in France the ministers were made by the king while in England they were made by parliament. The king had agreed to consult the nation regularly, to listen to their grievances and wishes, and to heed their suggestions in regard to the passing of new laws; but legislative initiative was his, and even the mode of consulting the nation – in other words the question of franchise – was for him to settle. On money matters consent of the nation's representatives was essential, but then property was involved, and the king could not compel his subjects to part with a portion of their wealth.

In Germany the ambiguous pledge of constitutions, contained in the 1815 treaty setting up the German Confederation, was not honoured by Prussia and other states. The rulers of the southern states – Bavaria, Baden and Württemberg – did grant constitutions modelled on the French Charter, and some form of national representation; but there the reason was one of self-preservation. The rulers could hardly invoke dynastic legitimacy after the buffeting which the dynastic principle had received in Germany under Napoleon, when over 300 of the 350 states of the old Reich had ceased to exist. These southern states simply lacked a principle of cohesion, and it was thought that parliamentary institutions, a share in the affairs of the country, and, it is only fair to add, the cultural and often artistic values and institutions cultivated by the princes (to mention only the glories of Munich and Dresden) would engender a sentiment of loyalty and serve as a focus of identity.

Prussia was in a different category. Treitschke is right in saying that Prussia was indeed the creation of its dynasty. No other dynasty in Europe, not even the Bourbons or Habsburgs, could claim to have created their dominions in the same way as the Hohenzollerns had, step by step, put together disparate territories and then welded them into a single whole. They were helped by an army under almost hereditary leadership and a bureaucracy which owed all its loyalty to the king and took pride in serving him and the Prussian state. The Prussian kings would not hear of a written constitution. On his accession to the throne the eloquent and romantic Frederick

15　Louis XVIII

William IV granted a relaxation of censorship and publicity of debates in the diets, and made arrangements for a meeting of a commission of the provincial estates every two years in Berlin. But on the eve of the 1848 Revolution he still angrily rejected the idea of having a piece of paper – a written constitution – put between him, the divinely appointed father of the nation, and his subjects to define obligations and to formalize in bloodless abstractions, permeated by the spirit of mean calculating suspicion, a direct, vital, rich and loving relationship.

In 1823 provincial estates – not a parliament of nationally elected deputies – were established in Prussia. A national parliament was bound to conjure up the spectre of the French national assembly and the claims of popular sovereignty. The Prussian conservatives would pull their noses: 'Nation – das klingt jakobinisch.' Instead of a homogeneous nation of equal citizens expressing a national will, there were to be estates, regional interests, elected local councils (as set up by Stein) to whom the king was willing to give a hearing. But as such they could not of course put forward a claim to sovereign legislative power. Metternich wrote:

The faction tries to implant the modern idea of popular sovereignty disguised under the form of the representative system. That is what constitutes – and H.M. the Emperor [Francis I] is intimately convinced of it – the principal agent of disorganization now spreading from one neighbouring power to another. That is the prime cause of the encroachments on the rights of sovereign authority of the German princes. . . . All other symptoms, however striking, however alarming they may be, H.M. the Emperor considers merely as the inevitable results of the preponderance which this fatal theory has gained.

THE POLITICS OF PLOT AND RIOT

The whole period of 1815–48 was an age of plot, conspiracy, riot and revolt on the one hand, and repression, censorship and police rule on the other, varying in degree from country to country. What was to the régime in power legitimacy and law, was to the opposition coercion and arbitrary oppression. What the opposition regarded as their sacred rights, appeared to the ruling classes as the threat of mob violence and barbarous anarchy. But while up to 1830 the objectives of revolt were in the main limited and of a rather negative, one may say defensive, nature – the overthrow of oppressive rule – those after 1830 expanded into boundlessness: the enthronement of some preordained universal happiness and total justice, if necessary by using violence against the selfish and recalcitrant. In both cases the devotees of revolution – a small *élite* of brave and ardent men – felt themselves justified in acting without explicit authorization.

Everywhere in Europe after 1815 there were frustrated Napoleonic veterans. The new régimes had put them on half-pay or dismissed them as untrustworthy, replacing them with faithful ex-émigrés and royalists. Even where there were elected assemblies of a sort, a restricted franchise closed the avenues of a political career to them. Notwithstanding their rich past, these veterans were in most cases still in the prime of life. The Revolution and the Napoleonic epic had been the work of comparatively young men. By contrast, the Restoration régimes had a preference for old age; they were

16 The memorable events of the French Revolution and Napoleon's rise to power, 20 June 1789–1800

anxious to compensate the faithful for their sacrifices and sufferings, and feared the radicalism of youth. In France the minimum age of the elector was fixed at thirty, and of the deputy at forty.

Junior officers hatched the Italian revolts of 1820 in Naples, Modena and other places. They were the backbone of the Carbonari. They rebelled against Ferdinand VII in Spain. They made the Decembrist uprising in Russia and paid with their lives. They started the ill-fated Polish rebellion of 1830 against the Russians.

The other recruits of conspiracy and plot were students – the Burschenschaften in Germany, the Filomats and Filarets in Lithuania,

33

17, 18   Freedom of the press, as propagandized by Daumier (left), affected the Paris cobbler (right), who was better informed than ever before

the polytechnicians who flocked into the early secret or semi-secret societies in France. All these student groups were animated by high-minded romantic ideals of spiritual rebirth, and engaged in a cult of virtue.

A tremendous urge for self-expression and a passionate prophetic ardour were part of the Romantic ambience. The Romantics were the heirs of the eighteenth century in their belief that man was fundamentally good and the individual immensely important. To stifle his self-expression, to strangle his potentialities, was a heinous crime. Hence, for example, the tremendous importance attached to the freedom of the press. With all their cult of the emotional and irrational, the Romantics were deeply convinced of the power of the word. Since man was reasonable, he was sure to be persuaded by the right kind of argument. Oppressive governments were at one with the rebels in overestimating the effect of the written or spoken word. For the incessantly widening public of newspaper

19, 20   The politician was caricatured in 1815 as 'devouring' his newspapers (left), in spite of the censor whom Daumier later depicted on his hobby-horse shears (right)

readers the press had replaced the sermon in Church, and there was as yet no cinema or radio or similar modern media of communication and entertainment. Governments therefore spent their fury on newspapers, pamphlets and cartoons. Some, like those by Daumier, were indeed most effective and often vicious. Metternich kept asking himself 'whether society can exist along with the liberty of press, a scourge unknown to the world before the last half of the seventeenth century'. Bonald demanded a quarantine for new ideas. It was censorship more than anything else that gave the *coup de grâce* to the Restoration, when persecuted editors and harassed printers sent their employees out into the streets.

The Romantic intoxication of the plotters, the indifference of the masses, and the grave inhibitions of the respectable opposition politicians in the background were the reasons for the dismal failure of almost all the uprisings. Nothing is more symptomatic in this respect than the Hamletic behaviour of Prince de Carignano, the

35

future King Charles Albert of Piedmont. When Santarosa staged a revolt in 1821, Charles Albert countermanded the orders he had given several times in twenty-four hours, and in the end turned informer. The Polish rebellion in 1830 won an initial success, although the conspirators failed in their nocturnal attempt to assassinate the Grand Duke Constantine. The *élan* of the youthful rebels of the night of 29 November was in strong contrast to the reluctance of the gentry to free the peasants. They feared not merely to lose revenue, but also to unleash a monster. A revolution afraid of a *levée en masse* was of course doomed.

The spirit of rebellion in Germany found expression not in revolt but in the famous Wartburg Festival of 1817, held in memory of both Luther's theses and the Battle of Leipzig. It reached its climax when the flames consumed the powdered wig, symbol of the *ancien régime*, and the sergeant's baton, symbol of stupid militarism. While it was the Spanish revolt under General Riego – signally put down by French troops acting on behalf of the Holy Alliance – that started the 1820 chain of uprisings, it was at the other end of the Continent, in 1825, that the most remarkable of all the revolts of the period occurred – the Decembrist uprising in Russia. No rebellion of those years embodied such wide and far-reaching aims. The north, represented by Colonel Murariev, aimed at a federal constitutional monarchy; the south, under the leadership of Pestel, dreamed of a centralized and democratic Jacobin republic and thorough land reform. There is no saying how different mankind's history might have been in the last hundred and fifty years had that bold venture achieved success. As it was, the uprising of *élite* troops on the day of his accession to the throne had a traumatic effect on Nicholas I, and probably accounts for much of the cast-iron rigidity of his reign as well as his sense of mission as the guardian of legitimacy and order in Europe. It may also explain his grim resolve to maintain serfdom, although he knew it to be 'a great evil', because

21, 22 French medals of 1830 commemorating two important events of that year: the Polish rebellion (above) and the investiture of Louis-Philippe as Lieutenant-General of France

he was convinced that any tampering with it was sure to engender still worse evils in the form of an elemental *jacquerie*. Unlike elsewhere, social unrest in post-1815 Britain – Peterloo, the Blanketeers' march, the Cato Street conspiracy, agricultural rioting, Luddite machine-breaking – bore the character of a genuine spontaneous reflex of the hungry masses.

Two assassinations shook the governments of France and the German-speaking countries, and helped to turn Alexander I of Russia against liberal ideas. In 1820 the Duc de Berry, the sole direct heir of the Bourbon dynasty until his wife was discovered to be miraculously with child, was murdered. There was a wave of panic and repression. Individual liberties and freedom of the press were suspended, and a new electoral law introduced the double vote, the final ballot being reserved for the highest taxpayers. This again stimulated conspiracy, first by the Amis de la Vérité, then by the Charbonnerie and Chevaliers de la Liberté, coming to a climax in the military insurrections at Belfort, Saumur, La Rochelle and Colmar. In these Bonapartists and Republicans joined hands, while respectable leaders of the official opposition (Lafayette, for example) waited in the wings – ready to emerge as saviour-leaders in case of success, or to disavow an irresponsible venture in case of failure.

23   The Wartburg Festival of 1817. Radical students of the Burschenschaften burn the symbols of slavery and reaction

24, 25   The July Revolution, 1830. Left, *The Insurgent Grocer* by Daumier, who never forgave Louis-Philippe for the deceptions of his régime. Right, Delacroix's apotheosis of the Republic, *Liberty Leading the People*, for which the new government presented him with the *Légion d'honneur*

In 1819 the German poet Kotzebue, suspected of being an agent of the Holy Alliance and a Tsarist spy, was murdered by the student Sand, who belonged to the Jacobin wing of German radicalism. This was a landmark in German history after 1815. The resulting Carlsbad decrees turned the German Diet into a Committee of Public Safety of the dynastic order. The Burschenschaften were dissolved, the universities were put under strict control, and the press was subjected to a most severe censorship. Although Metternich failed to induce the southern states to rescind the constitutions they had granted, a federal commission was appointed to keep an eye on revolutionary activities. This amounted to exercising a kind of police control over the individual German states, thus changing the whole character of the Bund.

In France the legitimist-aristocratic régime of the Restoration was brought down in July 1830 by a riot which swelled into a revolution. The conflict between aristocratic-clerical traditionalism and bourgeois liberalism came to an end with the complete victory of the latter. The stage was set for a direct confrontation between middle-class property and the proletarian have-nots. Hardly had the alliance of the two estates won its victory over the common foe, when the first signs of scission became visible on all fronts, the internal political, the social and the international. The trauma of revolution was of paramount importance in the fall of the Bourbon monarchy and the split into bourgeois *juste milieu* and republican-socialist radicalism. 'You were too young to see the Revolution, gentlemen, and

39

I have unfortunately more experience of that than you,' Charles X told his ministers on hearing the disastrous election results of 1830. 'The first retreat made by my unhappy brother was the signal of his ruin.' The King decided to resist firmly and to issue the ill-fated ordinances. Chantelauze justified the introduction of preliminary censorship with the claim that a 'turbulent democracy' was trying through a vicious press to substitute itself for the 'legitimate government', prevent the King from exercising his 'essential prerogative . . . essential attribute of sovereignty. . . . The very Constitution of the State . . .' To which the 44 opposition deputies, under Thiers's leadership, replied that 'the lawful régime had been interrupted; that of force had begun. . . . Obedience was no longer a duty.' Notwithstanding the revolutionary language and defiance of censorship by the opposition papers – which appeared without authorization – the thirty deputies assembled in the house of Casimir Périer rejected the idea of armed insurrection, contenting themselves with the protest drafted by Guizot. The initiative passed into the hands of students, members of the dissolved Carbonari and veterans of Napoleon's army who set about organizing committees of insurrection and rallying the workers – whom their employers had virtually placed at the disposal of the revolt by proclaiming a lockout. As soon as the insurgents had conquered Paris, the bourgeois deputies and politicians decided to put themselves at the head of the revolution in order to tame it and prevent the republicans from gaining power. Lafayette was proclaimed Commander of the National Guard and a municipal commission was set up at the Hôtel de Ville, the traditional seat of the sovereign people in insurrection.

From them came the famous proclamation drafted by Thiers and Mignet, both historians of the French Revolution. After stating that Charles X, having shed French blood, must no longer return to Paris, it went on to warn the people that 'the Republic will expose us to terrible divisions, and embroil us with Europe', and to proclaim the Duc d'Orléans 'a prince devoted to the cause of the revolution'. When Charles X with a deep sigh ('Here I am in the situation in which my unhappy brother was in 1792') decided to withdraw the ordinances and appoint a new government, the

Municipal Commission in a poetic *quid pro quo* forbade the publication of the King's proclamation. The provisional government, as the Municipal Commission was renamed, copied the 'Glorious Revolution' of 1688 in England, stating that 'Charles X had ceased to reign in France' by hypocritically and fraudulently attacking the institutions and liberties of France and shedding French blood. 'You will have a government which will have its origin in you, your heroism . . . all classes will have the same rights.' The efforts of the extremists to proclaim a republic proved unavailing. The Duc d'Orléans appeared with Lafayette on the balcony of the Hôtel de Ville. They embraced against the *tricolore*. After some initial hostility the crowd assembled beneath gave the new King, still nominally only Lieutenant-Général, the popular acclamation. Lafayette summed up the change that had taken place as 'a popular throne, surrounded by republican institutions'.

The emergence of the masses as a political factor was a shock to middle-class leadership. As late as 22 July 1830 the opposition journal *National* still accused the Ultra Prime Minister Polignac of social demagoguery in trying to find support

in a nation different from that which reads newspapers, is stirred by the debates in the chambers, disposes of capital, commands industry and possesses land, [and of] descending into the lower layers of the population, where no opinions are to be found, where there is hardly any political discernment. . . . Thousands of good, decent, simple human beings . . . easy to deceive and to exasperate . . . live from day to day . . . struggling at every hour of their lives against need, who have neither the time nor the repose of body and spirit necessary for occasional reflection on how the government of this country is being run.

26  Medal of Charles X

The Republican leader and saint, Carrel, writing on the same subject on the morrow of the revolutionary events, frankly confessed:

Was there any question of the people in our affairs at the time? . . . There was plenty of excitement among us doctors, merchants, deputies, men of letters. . . . There was not the slightest suspicion of what was going on below us in the class deprived of political rights.

41

Neither ancestry nor birth, religion or class predetermines one's station in life; work, effort and talent are the levers by which man obtains his position in life. That was the essence of the anti-feudal revolution. To be quite consistent, inherited wealth should also have been swept away with the hereditary privileges, for only when all were given an absolutely equal start was equality of opportunity real. In the discussion of the Rights of Man and the Citizen in 1789, many conservatives warned of the social danger inherent in the very idea of a proclamation of the Rights of Man. But uppermost in the minds of the authors of the Declaration was the wish to do away with the feudal-medieval conception of property as a cluster of rights, a focus of claims of different parties and a trusteeship over which the community had certain suzerain powers for the common good. To them property was an extension of the natural faculties with which the individual came into the world, and with the help of which he realized himself by increasing it.

The contradiction between *carrière ouverte aux talents* and inherited property – the fundamental dichotomy of the bourgeois order – was epitomized in Napoleon's career. The little corporal was self-

27  Satire by Isabey (himself the figure at far left) of the *parvenu* society of the Directoire, 1798

28, 29   The famous 'corpse head' of Napoleon (left) – a German 'hieroglyphic portrait of the destroyer, with a parody of his titles'; and the Romantic image by David

made, and wished to impress the fact upon everybody at his coronation: when the Pope was about to crown him he took the crown from the Pope's hands and did it for himself. Well into the nineteenth century a young person dreaming aloud of future greatness would, when called back to earth from lunatic visions, retort, 'And did not Napoleon start as a corporal?' But the Emperor was set upon establishing a dynasty, and the hereditary principle of the Empire required a proper context, a hereditary nobility – not just a *Légion d'honneur* to exalt men who made good, but a hereditary nobility with a suitable income, and what is more, entails. Was the Empire a republic as its title implied, or a monarchy of the old type? It was neither. It was a newly conquered and reshaped France, in which the victor and his retainers, like the Franks who overran Roman Gaul, had founded a new dynasty and a new aristocracy.

Napoleon was casting about for some grains of granite, as he put it, round which the lava of revolutionary change could congeal in some solid social pattern of beliefs, customs, institutions. Religious faith was one of them, and another was property. The two were

43

not unconnected in the Emperor's mind. He was fond of saying that if the masses did not believe in God, there would be no reason for them not to rise and cut the throats of the rich. It was to be the Roman institution of property – the absolute *ius utendi et abutendi*, entirely unencumbered. Napoleon intended to make property appear as a prize for effort and a token of merit, not an inherited gift. At the same time he set great store on the family. Hereditary property and the family were seen as great stabilizers, imposing a discipline, a sense of responsibility, care for the future, interest in orderly continuity. The two together implied a hierarchical social framework. Thus even at this date, the position of the bourgeoisie was seen to be fraught with ambiguity. It was a revolutionary product, but its aim was stability. In the eyes of the Right it bore the seeds of its own destruction, and had to be saved from its suicidal urge.

Thus the third of the famous ordinances of the Polignac government, on the morrow of its resounding defeat in the general election of 1830, laid down that elections should take place in two stages, voters in *arrondissements* electing a quarter of the wealthiest among

30 This English satire shows the passing of the Reform Bill as the last triumphant scene of a play, with the audience applauding from the stalls and gallery

them to sit in the departmental colleges, which were to elect the deputies. Only payment of land tax and other property taxes was to be taken into account as a qualification to be an elector or candidate for election, and patents and door and window taxes were excluded. This meant that a considerable part of the industrial and intellectual bourgeoisie would be deprived of the franchise it had had since 1815. The ensuing revolution – and the wholly bourgeois order that emerged into an electorate enlarged from some 100,000 to nearly a quarter of a million – marked the conquest of power by property. As will be shown later, this effected profound changes in bourgeois ideology.

In England, too, the Right warned the middle-class reformers that it was unwise to open the floodgates. Some Tories, it is true, had had thoughts of reform – if only because of the crushing costs of elections, which the moneyed interest could bear better than the landed interest. But the disaster that befell the Bourbons frightened them into taking a determined stand against subversive principles.

The Ultras in France had argued that any retreat from the most rigid divine-right principle, any concession to demands for popular representation and constitutional guarantees, meant taking the first step towards a republic which would lead to communism. In England the diehard Tories similarly feared that any departure from the historic franchise – even when it was as absurd and corrupt as at Old Sarum – was bound to lead to universal suffrage, and consequently to social revolution. This was the position when the debate on the Great Reform Bill of 1832 began.

The opponents of the Bill again and again warned the reformers that any tampering with the existing franchise meant letting loose what the Duke of Wellington called fierce democracy; and that, as France had shown, inevitably degenerated into terrorist anarchy followed by military tyranny. Political rights were on a different plane from the natural rights of the individual, which were concerned with safeguards against arbitrary oppression, but did not extend to a share in power. For partnership in the running of the commonwealth special qualifications and faculties were required: a stake in the country, a sense of responsibility, certain businesslike qualities, and a measure of education and experience; none of these were possessed by the propertyless and uneducated.

These arguments were not denied by middle-class politicians. Lord John Russell, the chief spokesman of the supporters of the Bill, had one reply. The proposed Bill was going to increase the number of men interested in the preservation of property and political stability. It would make property more secure, and less vulnerable than when the vote was a monopoly of narrow groups, and important interests were excluded from a share in national responsibility. In brief, the Whigs believed that they were going, in the words of Macaulay, 'to save property divided against itself, save the multitude, endangered by its own ungovernable passions . . . aristocracy endangered by its own power. . . .' This was countered by a no less telling argument from the opposite benches. What guarantee was there that the proposed Bill would secure finality – that there would be no pressure for a further extension of the franchise, and eventually for that universal suffrage which neither Tory nor Whig wanted? Was there anything sacred or final about the £10 test? Why not £8, or £5, or none at all?

In all the discussions at Westminster no reference was made to the right to vote as a natural right. This was due not only to the pragmatic temper and empirical tradition of English politics, but to the fact that at the time hardly anyone advocated universal suffrage; and, obviously, recognition of a natural right to vote meant granting universal suffrage.

The inherited privilege of property was turning the bourgeois order into a neo-feudalism, with inherited wealth facing inherited poverty. Tocqueville saw very clearly the vulnerability of the bourgeois position. In the past, property was only one of the privileges, and it was thus protected by clusters of other inequalities. With the abolition of all other inequalities, inequality of wealth became a conspicuous injustice. Furthermore, it was calculated to make equality before the law illusory, or at least unimportant. The liberal thinker prophesied that all future revolts would be uprisings against property. Marx branded bourgeois deceit in proclaiming property irrelevant to politics by sanctifying it as a natural right with which the state could not properly interfere. It had, on the contrary, become the one great issue, whereas bourgeois politics was merely a game between Ins and Outs. Bourgeois insistence on eternal, universal, inalienable natural rights was simply a ruse designed to grant such status to property. The bourgeois parliamentary system – with its narrow franchise – was only an organization of property-holders designed to ensure the best conditions for the preservation and increase of their property.

The Declaration of the Rights of Man of 1789 failed to mention any right to social assistance, education, or work, all things to be found in the 1793 Declaration, which became the rallying cry of the Left in the first half of the nineteenth century. The Declaration of 1789 was drafted by men who seem to have lived in no fear of unemployment, poverty and disease, and were not worried about getting an education for their children. They were simply unaware of these scourges, and therefore felt no need to put them into the social contract. The Declaration is concerned with the possibility of free self-expression by the individual and with the organization of government in such a way as to make the violation or restriction of such self-expression impossible. It envisages men on their feet, ready for the race – it does not consider it to be its task to put them there. Thus far the Declaration is the expression of the bourgeois mentality, and indeed constitutes its act of self-determination.

Both bourgeois liberalism and proletarian socialism shared the underlying assumption of a system of universal social harmony that would one day reconcile individual happiness with the general good. In the eyes of the liberals that natural tendency was vitiated by the monopolistic parasitism of the landlords, the obtuse indolence of tradition-bound forces, and the rapacious avarice of the ignorant and the short-sighted. In the eyes of the followers of Adam Smith and Bentham, a hidden hand would ensure universal harmony if free economic initiative was not interfered with. The less government, the better. On the other hand, the logic of an industrial civilization did not stop at pulling down feudal-absolutist paternalism in order to remove obstacles from economic endeavour. It carried with it the demand for a rational organization of society.

47

In most parts of Europe the struggle against feudal survivals was an aspect, and even a condition, of modernization. In England and Germany, though not for the same reason, the squire was not merely a landlord, but the focus of local government, holding judicial, administrative and police powers. He was not simply a nominee of the government, nor was he elected by the population. He was unpaid and therefore had to be well-to-do. In his independence he embodied and symbolized a decentralized administration. The gentry carried a good deal of responsibility for the maintenance of the poor and even some form of popular education. Privilege was thus a kind of reward for burden, and burden the price of special status. Poor communications, great local diversity, lack of expert knowledge and of funds were the reasons why even a highly centralized state like Prussia and a despotism like Russia were content to leave the administration of local affairs in the hands of the landlords. It was of course part of a tacit bargain between kings and nobility, while in England it was part of the Whig preponderance, and of a system designed to curtail the scope of central government.

France became a modern state under Napoleon, who was able to build on the foundations of Bourbon centralization, which was continued in a different form, and was even strengthened by the ideology of 'la République une et indivisible' and the conditions of terrorist dictatorship at war.

In England the struggle against the privileged position of the landed interest was not only a middle-class concern, but in the last resort a struggle for the modernization of Britain. The Reform Bill of 1832 deprived the landowning classes of their preponderant political position. After this it was unfair to leave the burden of the Poor Law on their shoulders. The countryside bore a disproportionate part of it once industry had begun to attract large numbers to towns, for the migrants continued to figure on the poor law roll in their village of birth. Hence the new Poor Law system of 1834. Once the state took over Poor Law administration, the old institution of the Justice of Peace was on the way towards being dismantled. More and more duties and prerogatives had to be assumed by the central government, and for reasons of efficiency and economy they had to be administered from the centre by paid full-time experts and officials. By stages, slowly and in a rather muddled way, police, education, public health became the concerns of Whitehall. With the venerable JPs went the oligarchic corporations entrenched in the local government councils of towns and cities, to be replaced by more or less democratically elected bodies. In short, local inherited privilege was replaced by bureaucratic state centralization or local election. Once the landed aristocracy and gentry were released from their special obligations, economic privilege in the form of the Corn Laws appeared the more unjustifiable, and the Conservative argument that high tariffs on imported corn were necessary to preserve the backbone of England, carried no more conviction than did the warnings of famine and disaster to come in this age of railways, steamships and mounting foreign trade figures. It was characteristically the Tory party under Peel that gave reality to the trend towards rational uniformity – in place of the diversity of custom, precedent and privilege – which first triumphed in the Reform Bill of 1832 under the Whigs.

The struggle for the triumph of rational and utilitarian criteria could hardly be dissociated from the struggle for power. In England the philosophical radicals quite early concluded that, men being what they were, a narrow franchise was bound to result in the privileged few caring not for the greatest happiness of the greatest number, but for the greatest happiness of their own restricted number. The radicals were thus led to support the democratic idea of universal suffrage.

In Prussia – to take another example – the crisis of 1847–8 arose out of the refusal of the bourgeois deputies to vote a loan for the construction of the Berlin–Koenigsberg railway – a most progressive and economically important scheme – unless the royal government agreed to turn the united Landtag into a regular national parliament. This lack of confidence in the ability of the old-fashioned monarchy and Junkers to guide the destinies of an increasingly more industrial society was the first step towards a demand by the bourgeoisie for power to do it themselves.

31, 32   The poor in Britain seemed as oppressed as ever in the 1830s and 1840s, in contrast to the rich capitalist, his yawning dogs and his pampered monkey. Parish poor relief (below) was begrudging and humiliating

The refusal of the forces of yesterday to yield to bourgeois demands appeared as a resolve to continue a régime of oppression and exploitation and as a bar to social harmony. The Declaration of 1789 had solemnly proclaimed the right to oppose oppression, indeed enunciated the duty to resist it. For otherwise the revolt of the Third Estate against royalty had been nothing but a crime. The Fourth Estate took the Third Estate at its word, and turned the tables upon bourgeois liberalism.

The rationalist philosophy and the French Revolution had proclaimed the rights of man and promised equality. And from then onwards not only burdens and humiliations which had previously been borne as an inescapable fate of that station of life in which it had pleased heaven to place one, but any injury to what came to be thought of as the dignity of man, began to appear as intolerable, and justifying resistance.

As has already been pointed out, the idea of rights was in the eyes of both camps anchored to a general vague vision of a harmonious state of society, which was allegedly Nature's intention. It was only natural to draw the conclusion that so long as harmony had not been enthroned, there was disorder in the world, of which some forces were the author and beneficiary.

ORIGINS

Socialism became the common denominator for all those creeds and movements in the first half of the nineteenth century which purported to offer a social system based on justice and reason, as an alternative to the social systems of the past all of which allegedly derived from selfish violence and were drifting with no compass. The common aim of all socialist trends was to create conditions which would allow man a maximum of self-expression and at the same time secure the highest measure of social integration. The rights of man and the general good, freedom and organization – their reconciliation was to mark the beginning of real history, the enthronement of a social order of absolute and final validity. While the postulate was there before the French Revolution, in the form of the 'natural order', the great upheaval beginning in 1789 was to the believers a lesson that their dream was not just the idle *jeu d'esprit* of a few isolated thinkers, but a force calculated to move millions and become flesh in laws and institutions.

The Revolution laid the foundations for the liberal bourgeois system based on property, but it also initiated the socialist tradition as a leaven which has been at work in the world ever since. Fairly early in the Revolution both logic and pressure of circumstances posed the problem of making the abstract and purely legal idea of freedom real by translating it into a guaranteed existence through ownership of property, secure employment or social assistance. The state was soon led to subordinate the absolute rights of private property to the needs of the body social, so that the weaker members could be adequately helped. Such measures as the abolition of feudalism and the confiscation of Church property were followed under the stress of war and scarcity by economic dictatorship: fixing of prices, forms of rationing, and indeed class policies designed to make the rich pay for the maintenance of the poor, and for their own subjection to armed forces manned by the under-privileged. At an earlier date liberty had already been considered incomplete and insecure without equality, and laws had been demanded to limit the amount of property a single individual could hold. The eventual identification of poverty with loyalty to the Republic and of wealth with counter-revolutionary attitudes, suggested to men with a strong inclination to generalize immediate experiences into eternal truths the vision of a universal struggle between the haves and the have-nots. The refusal of the privileged to give up their long-established positions was interpreted as proof that a social transformation was impossible without coercive violence: without a revolutionary government in the language of Robespierre and Saint-Just or without a revolutionary dictatorship in that of Babeuf.

33, 34, 35
Three revolutionaries.
Robespierre,
Saint-Just (centre),
and Babeuf

Babeuf had also reached the conclusion that the absolute mechanical equality he so much desired was unattainable without common ownership and a strictly uniform education.

French thought and the revolutionary experience of France had their parallel in England. British thinkers, from Locke to Ricardo and his disciples, whether liberal or socialist, were more concerned with the definition of the right of property than with the abstract notion of right. They also felt more strongly than the French – or at least at an earlier date – the urge to re-examine their thinking in the light of the Industrial Revolution. Locke, the father of European liberalism, sought justification for private property in the labour invested to appropriate a portion of the bounties of nature. While setting no limits to man's successful exertions to increase his possessions – with the help of family and servants – as much as possible, Locke denied the right of the proprietor to amass an excess that would be doomed to rot away. The philosopher took for granted the right to bequeath and inherit the fruits of one's industry, since he regarded a man's descendants as extensions of his personality. What was no less important, he set no limit to the right of the proprietor to turn the things appropriated by him into indestructible gold – i.e. money – as capital for further economic endeavour which would benefit everybody.

53

Adam Smith based himself entirely on Locke, but paid less attention to property rights in themselves than to the dynamic relationship between individual economic activity and the workings of the social organism or, more accurately, the national economy. The mechanism of exchange, derived from man's primordial and indestructible instinct of barter, became the keystone of his system. A 'hidden hand' ensured an equitable exchange of equivalent products of labour in such a way that private vices – the acquisitive urge and selfish calculation – were turned into public virtues promoting general well-being through their contribution to the smooth functioning of the mechanism of exchange as a whole.

Thus where the French Revolutionary experience suggested regulation from above, British liberal philosophy put its hopes in a kind of predetermined natural harmony, not to be interfered with artificially by legislators. Adam Smith, and of course Locke, thought primarily in terms of independent self-reliant producers engaged in free exchange. The Industrial Revolution revealed the producer as an entrepreneur with power of initiative and capital at his disposal, flanked on one side by the hereditary owner of land – a monopolist who extracted rent for the use of his land by producers – and on

36, 37, 38 Capitalism creates wealth. Nathan Rothschild (left) was the London representative of the powerful financier family, and its first baron. Adam Smith, shown above on the obverse of a Scottish penny; his *The Wealth of Nations* (1776) is commemorated on the reverse

39 Caricature of English speculators, investing in a variety of schemes for quick money on 'The Road to Ruin'

the other by workers, who had only hands, and no independent initiative or tools of their own. The landlord appeared to be a burden on the productive effort, since he exacted rent without making any contribution towards increasing production, while workers were reduced to the status of a commodity to be paid for – and paid just enough to stay fit as an instrument. The inordinate multiplication of human beings – Malthus claimed – was creating an over-supply of hands, while cut-throat competition between producers made an increase in wages impossible. It was the entrepreneurs' initiative, skill and readiness to take risks that created all wealth, particularly capital for further industrial activity.

The socialists regarded capital as the accumulated fruits of the workers' labour, which the employers appropriated after paying them subsistence wages. The real producers of wealth were the workers. The value of the product was equivalent to the labour in-vested in it. Consequently the worker had a right to the integral produce of his labour.

The misery of the urban worker was a new phenomenon. Famine engendered by natural scarcity had been accepted as inevitable, but poverty in the midst of plenty appeared a scandal without precedent.

55

By then men were habituated to the idea of equal rights, and many accepted Jeremy Bentham's formula of 'the greatest happiness for the greatest number'. But technological developments also seemed to promise infinite bounty, and to belie ancient fears of inevitable scarcity. The marvellous scientific cohesion underlying the mechanism of division of labour and industrial organization made economic anarchy, recurrent crises and the misery of the workers seem particularly revolting. The liberal philosophy of non-interference with the workings of the social mechanism lest the natural tendency towards natural harmony be disturbed, appeared to the weak to be a rationalization of the selfish interest of the strong who would not be interfered with.

In the course of its polemic against the claims of the lower orders, the bourgeoisie was driven to develop a set of arguments which seemed to contradict its own original tenets, and to reaffirm quite a few reactionary and counter-revolutionary ideas. Not only would freedom be jettisoned, if the state were called upon to provide for the needs of the poor, and thus driven to take over the whole economy of the country; civilization itself would be gravely endangered. For men exerted themselves only under the stress of need, and once free of care they would simply grow sluggish and lazy and multiply without restraint. A situation would thus be created in which too many mouths have too little to eat. Here was a denial of the sacred articles of the bourgeois creed – the goodness and perfectibility of man, a return to a kind of original sin philosophy, and a rejection of the optimistic idea of social harmony and uninterrupted progress. The few were confirmed in their right to make use of the toil of the many in order to produce and maintain a sample of civilization. To this was added indignation with the 'terribles simplificateurs' who believed that they could make and unmake old established societies, with the help of a few abstract formulae, without regard to historic tradition, peculiar national character, and other empirical circumstances. But then, the Third Estate itself had earlier on been accused precisely of that.

The various socialist schools of the age lend themselves to a classification different from the one that has become a common-

No. 11. Vol. III.] SATURDAY, NOVEMBER 9, 1833. [Price 1½d.

THE CRISIS

AND

NATIONAL CO-OPERATIVE TRADES' UNION AND EQUITABLE LABOUR EXCHANGE GAZETTE

40 Heading of Robert Owen's periodical *The Crisis*, 1833, which contrasts two ways of life

place – Utopian and 'scientific' socialism. There was first the purely totalitarian-democratic trend represented by the heirs of extreme Jacobinism – such men as Babeuf, Buonarroti and Blanqui. To them absolute equality was the embodiment of justice and the goal of all history. The enlightened vanguard was therefore justified in hastening The Day by all means, the best – because most rapid – being a violent *coup*. Once the selfish and unregenerate had been forcibly eliminated, proper social arrangements and a suitable system of education would quickly bring about a régime of perfect communist equality and complete unanimity – in other words, a true democracy in which all are free and equal because all are animated by the same sentiments.

The prophets of the other school were Robert Owen, Fourier and to some extent also Louis Blanc and Proudhon. They fought shy of the idea of violently imposing collective patterns from above; and they feared any form of centralization as inimical to true liberty and dangerous to the ideal of justice based on the worker's right to the integral produce of his labour. Owen and Fourier therefore spun visions of small self-contained co-operative communities based on a perfect division of labour. Owen and his followers believed for a while in a union of all Trade Unions, and tried to set one up. They hoped it would evolve into a federation of producers' and consumers' co-operatives which would inexorably and peacefully absorb capitalist organizations, until capitalism itself withered away. While the Owenites preached the sacred principle of self-help, Louis Blanc, like Lassalle later, expected the existing state to finance

57

workers' co-operatives, thus somewhat surprisingly hoping that the capitalist state would pay for its own burial. Proudhon's anarchism envisaged neither collectivist organizations of any kind nor state aid in any form. The credit necessary for setting up small producers – heads of families – free from the bondage of usury, and for ensuring an equitable exchange of the products of labour, was to be got on a voluntary basis.

Justice, not historical necessity, was uppermost in the minds of these thinkers. This is not to say that they regarded their systems as purely artificial contrivances. On the contrary, they insisted quite firmly that circumstances and historical developments played a part in suggesting their ideas, and indeed were considered both necessary and feasible. But it was Saint-Simon and his school who were most impressed by the inexorable imperatives inherent in technological and social evolution; their thought is a convenient starting-point from which to discuss the development of socialist ideas and the significance of socialism as a political force on the eve of 1848.

ROMANTIC TECHNOCRACY

Saint-Simon, the cosmopolitan aristocratic adventurer, was brought up to think himself destined for an exceptional fate. Indeed, when hardly out of adolescence he became a colonel in the American army fighting for independence, and was the author of a crop of astonishing plans for mighty undertakings such as a Panama canal, and waterways and roads in Spain and Holland. Yet with all his passion to improve man's lot by subduing nature with the help of human ingenuity, Saint-Simon remained a passive observer at the time of the French Revolution, although he renounced his aristocratic title and assumed the name of Bonhomme. The Revolution became to him an occasion for wild financial speculation which at first made him rich, then desperately poor, and finally landed him in prison.

Saint-Simon's earliest pamphlet, *A Letter from a Citizen of Geneva*, contains the bizarre scheme of a Council of Newton. The finest savants of Europe were to assemble in a mausoleum erected in honour of the great scientist, and deliberate on the problems of society. The author thereby gave picturesque expression to his view

41 Comte de
Saint-Simon

that in the French Revolution popular sovereignty had proved itself as fumbling, erratic and wrong as the divine right of kings, and that the tenets of rationalism about the rights of man, liberty and equality, had shown themselves just as irrelevant to man's problems as theological doctrine. Not being rooted in any certainty comparable to that of science, old and new political ideas alike became only a pretext for the will of one set of men to dominate all others – which was all, in fact, that politics had ever been.

What had made men yield to such palpable errors for so long and then caused Saint-Simon to see through them at precisely that moment? Unlike eighteenth-century philosophers – such as his masters Turgot and Condorcet – Saint-Simon does not invoke the march of progress, the victory of enlightenment, or the sudden resolve of men. He points to the importance assumed by scientific advance, technological development and problems of industrial production, all based upon scientific precision, verifiable facts and quantitative measurements which left no room for human arbitrariness.

In the past, mythological and theological modes of thought, medieval notions of chivalry, metaphysical preoccupations and so on were the accompaniment – or, as Saint-Simon more often seems to suggest, the matrix – of the economic conditions and the social-political order of the day. In brief, frames of mind, modes of production and social political systems hang together, and develop together, and the stages of such overall development cannot be skipped. The industrial system which the nineteenth century was ushering in had its beginnings in the Middle Ages. Within the womb of a civilization dominated by priests and warriors, shaped by values and expectations not of this world, geared for war and inspired by theatrical sentiments of chivalry, there began a mighty collective effort to fashion things, instruments and values designed to enhance men's lives here and now : industrial production, economic exchange and scientific endeavour. The communes had at first no thought of subverting the feudal-theological order, within which they made their earliest steps – firstly because they were as yet too weak for such a revolt, and secondly because they did not value the external accoutrements of power. They believed only in positive tangible goods and solid achievements in the social-economic and scientific domain.

This was the cause of a divorce between content and form. While in external appearance warriors and priests still held the reins of authority, real power was increasingly concentrated in the hands of the productive classes. These classes, whose position, indeed whose very existence, lacked acknowledged legitimacy in the official scheme of things, developed a special ethos. Knowing the ruling classes to be incompetent to deal with matters of decisive importance to them, the bourgeoisie resorted to a theory of *laissez-faire* which condemned all government interference and glorified individual initiative and the interplay of economic interests. In order to clothe this class interest in theoretical garb, bourgeois spokesmen evolved the doctrine of the natural rights of man and the theory of checks and balances and division of power. These were designed to curb the power-drives of the feudal forces, and indeed succeeded in undermining the self-assurance of the aristocratic order.

In Saint-Simon's view, the French Revolution signified not so much the triumph of rationalist-democratic ideas as the total victory of the productive classes and the final swamping of feudal-theological values by positive forces. But this fundamental fact was distorted and obscured by those metaphysicians and lawyers who, having played an important part in helping the industrial classes to win, mistook their secondary role for a mission to impose their ideas and their rule upon society. Instead of stepping aside and letting the imperatives of industrial endeavour shape new institutions, they set out to impose their conjectural ideas upon society, side-tracking the real issues and befogging them with rhetoric and sophistry. In effect their intention was not to abolish the old system which divided society into rulers and ruled, but to continue it, only substituting themselves for the feudal lords; in other words, to rule by force. For where the relationship between rulers and ruled is not grounded in the nature of things as is that, for example, between doctor and patient, teacher and pupil – that is, on a division of functions – the only reality is the rule of man over man based on force. This form of relationship dated from the days when man was considered to need protection by superiors because he was weak, lowly and ignorant, or had to be kept from mischief because he was riotous and savage. It was no longer justified once the Revolution had proved that man had come of age. It was time for government, in other words the state, to make room for an administration of *things*, and conscious, sustained planning of the national economy. The need to keep law and order, allegedly always so pressing and relentless, would be reduced to a minimum when social relations were derived from objective necessities. The whole problem was thus reduced to the discovery of the 'force of things', the requirements of the mechanism of production. Once these had become the measure of all things, there would be no room for the distinction between rulers and ruled in the traditional political sense. The nexus of all human relationships would be the bond between expert knowledge and experience on the one hand, and discipleship, fulfilment of necessary tasks, on the other. The whole question of liberty and equality would then assume a quite different significance.

In fact men would no longer experience the old acute craving for liberty and equality. A scientific apportioning of functions would ensure perfect cohesion of the totality, and the high degree of integration would draw the maximum potential from every participant in the collective effort. Smooth, well-adjusted participation heightens energy and stills any sense of discomfort or malaise. There is no yearning for freedom and no wish to break away in an orchestra, a choir, a rowing boat. Where parts do not fit and abilities go to waste, there is a sense of frustration and consequently oppression, and man longs to get away. The question of equality would not arise once inequality was the outcome of a necessary and therefore just division of tasks. There is no inequality where there is no domination for the sake of domination.

Such a perfect integration remained to be discovered. Pursuing his quest, Saint-Simon stumbled upon socialism, and then found himself driven to religion. Waste, frustration, deprivation, oppression were the denial of both cohesion of the whole and the self-expression of the individual. Those scourges were epitomized in the existence of the poorest and most numerous class – the workers. And so what started with Saint-Simon as a quest for positive certainty and efficiency gradually assumed the character of a crusade on behalf of the disinherited, the underprivileged and frustrated. The integrated industrial productive effort began to appear as conditioned upon the abolition of poverty, and dialectically the abolition of poverty now seemed the real goal of a fully integrated collective endeavour.

But was the removal of friction and waste enough to ensure the smooth working of the whole? And would rational understanding suffice to ensure wholehearted participation in the collective effort? Saint-Simon was led to face at a very early stage of socialism the question of incentives. He felt that mechanical, clever contrivances, intellectual comprehension and enlightened self-interest were in themselves insufficient as incentives and motives. And so the positivist, despising mythical, theological and metaphysical modes of thought, by degrees evolved into a mystical Romantic. He became acutely aware of the need for incentives stronger, more impelling and compelling than reason and utility. In a sense he had already come to grips with the problem in the famous distinction between organic and critical epochs in history, a distinction which was destined to become so important in the theory of his disciple, Auguste Comte.

These two types of epoch alternate in history. There is a time of harmony and concord, like the pre-Socratic age in Greece and the Christian Middle Ages, and there are times of disharmony and discord, like post-Socratic Greece and the modern age, which began with the Reformation, evolved into rationalism, and came to a climax in the French Revolution. The organic ages are periods of a strong and general faith, when the basic assumptions comprise a harmonious pattern and are unquestioningly taken for granted. There are no dichotomies of any kind, and classes live in harmony. In the critical ages there is no longer any consensus about basic assumptions; beliefs clash, traditions are undermined, there is no accepted image of the world. Society is torn by class war and selfishness is rampant.

The crying need of the new industrial age was for a new religion. There must be a central principle to ensure integration of all the particular truths and a single impulse for all the diverse spiritual endeavours. The sense of unity of life must be restored, and every person must be filled with such an intense propelling and life-giving sense of belonging to that unity, that he would be drawn to the centre by the chains of love, and stimulated by a joyous irresistible urge to exert himself on behalf of all.

Saint-Simon called this new religion of his 'Nouveau Christianisme'. It was to be a real fulfilment of the original promise of Christianity, and was to restore that unity of life which traditional Christianity – decayed and distorted – had done its best to deny and destroy. The concept of original sin had led to a pernicious separation of mankind into a hierarchy of the perfect and the mass of simple believers. This carried with it the distinction between theory and practice, the perfect bliss above and the vale of tears below; the result was compromise and reconciliation with – in effect, approval of – evil here and now.

The disciples of Saint-Simon created an all-embracing doctrine from the socialist and religious premises of their master, and claimed for it a significance as epoch-making as that of Christianity eighteen centuries earlier. To us, however, it represents a version of social Romanticism run riot.

The master concerned himself with producers on the one hand, and on the other with parasitic idlers like soldiers, priests and lawyers. He included among producers property-owners and bankers as well as industrialists, savants and workers, and he hailed the bankers especially as the natural planners in a modern industrial society. But his followers gradually came to condemn the whole bourgeoisie as a class. They did this after making an acute analysis of liberal economic doctrines. Their analysis was much the same as that of Fourier, and of such early British socialists as Hodgskin, Thompson and Bray. They found it easy to prove that the liberal régime of *laissez-faire* had replaced one type of feudalism by another, namely that of inherited property and inherited poverty. They repudiated the idea of the 'hidden hand', arguing that the capitalist and the worker were not bartering on equal terms. To Saint-Simon himself, property was an instrument of production, and the right to it was conditioned upon the proper use made of it on behalf of and to the benefit of society. The institution of private property was not in itself an evil, and common ownership was not an absolute good or an end in itself. But Saint-Simon's disciples reached the conclusion that society alone was qualified to decide how the instruments of production should be used, since this depended on the overall plan; social organization of production implied social ownership of the tools.

The master and his school were optimists. In their view socialism had been in the making for centuries. The medieval communes had played their part by taking wealth from idle nobles and transforming it into an instrument of production. Even the usury practised by Jews and Lombards had contributed by sucking the feudal lords dry and putting their possessions into circulation in the form of commercial and industrial credit. Taxation, estate duties, the power of

public authorities to requisition private property with or without compensation – all of these had represented a kind of creeping socialism. A stage had now been reached at which a simple ukase nationalizing all property, coupled with a promise of life-long rent to the present owners and possibly their immediate descendants, would suffice to establish social ownership.

The problem of cohesion and permanence, in other words of motives and incentives, had therefore become more acute. Saint-Simon's school started by putting all its emphasis upon the right of every individual to realize his potentialities, and upon the vibrating, all-pervading sense of the oneness of life. This sense appeared to be the essential condition of self-realization, and was not a matter of intellectual comprehension but of a life-giving feeling and *élan*. It would not be possessed by everybody in the same degree. Those who had the greatest capacity for universal love and the ability to inspire it in others would be called priests, prophets, poets, seers. Their power of imparting enthusiasm to others, of sweeping others along with them, accorded them the dignity and role of natural leaders. They became as a consequence even more important than technocrats or chiefs of production. The bond between leaders of this religious type and those led by them was not a bond of authority and subordination but of love given and love taken, of joyous partnership in a great experience. Those in need of guidance must cherish their priestly leaders with a submissive ardent love. Only then would the leaders feel truly inspired and, their abilities thus enhanced, would discharge their task more effectively. Since the relationship was dynamic and direct, and each situation was unique, there was no possibility of laying down in advance laws and pre-scriptions for all possible cases. Living experience could not be con-tained in a formula and ossified into a typical case. This realization lay behind the Saint-Simonist idea of the 'loi vivante'. The leader-prophet-artist was not bound by any written code of laws. He was the living law; his immediate intuitive responses created the law in given situations.

The Saint-Simonist school evolved from an apostolic community, spreading the gospel with missionary and prophetic zeal, into a quasi-monastic establishment and school of character. Here disciples

42,43   Romantic technocracy. The Saint-Simonian community at Ménilmontant, based on the philosophy of 'each according to his abilities' (above), was headed by Father Enfantin (right)

were prepared for the great task of converting mankind simultaneously into an industrial workshop and a confraternity of believers.

In the community the cult of personality – of the two popes, Enfantin and Bazard – was carried to bizarre lengths, with the help of artistic symbolism, religious rites and hierarchical paraphernalia.

As the unregenerate world showed scant eagerness to be converted (in spite of the powerful impact of the new religion on some of the finest spirits of the age), romantic mysticism enveloped the sect, pitching its expectations and emotions to the highest key. Rejection of the dichotomies stemming from the doctrine of original sin led beyond the unity of life to the affirmation of all instincts and urges as good and deserving fulfilment. The rehabilitation of woman, the senses and the flesh assumed the character of a test of faith, and eventually became the focal point of the whole movement. Universal brotherhood and love were not in any case compatible with the

existence of the self-contained private family. Furthermore, the universal redemption preached by the Saint-Simonists called for the liberation of woman. Paternity was to be the exclusive secret of the mother. When those who could not bring themselves to go so far broke away, Enfantin proclaimed the issue to be the ultimate test of the capacity for redemption by the religion of love and emancipation from the old bonds. Moreover, the vision of redemption was now epitomized in the Woman-Messiah who was soon to emerge and undo what Mother Eve had done. Eve had led mankind into sin and perdition; the Woman-Messiah was to perform the role of a second Christ, this time by bringing complete salvation, setting free all man's instincts and urges, and proclaiming them as good and noble and life-giving.

These excesses doomed the movement. In spite of the strong impact it had on poets and artists, Saint-Simonist pantheism soon

44
Caricature of Berlioz conducting,
1846

died out, and remained no more than a curiosity, a striking expression of a mood. Nor did the activities of the school as a socialist group leave much trace. But the influence of their teachings was profound and lasting. The technocratic aspect of the movement found great scope in the immediate future. The Saint-Simonist visionaries soon became the architects of French capitalism, the planners and entrepreneurs who set about covering France with a network of railways and piercing it with canals, building up a banking system based on modern methods of credit, and initiating many industrial ventures. Their schemes for developing the other continents found some realization in public works in Egypt and Algeria, and indeed in the Suez Canal: Lesseps himself passed through a Saint-Simonist spell in his youth. Nor should it be forgotten that Saint-Simonist views on the social role of art and the unity of life captured the imagination and quickened the pen of Heine and Mazzini, Berlioz and Alfred de Vigny, Carlyle and Michelet.

## UTOPIA

Fourier, the lonely, half-crazy old bachelor sunk in dreams, represents another method of grappling with the twin problems of social integration and individual self-expression. As indicated earlier, there was a much stronger dose of pre-Revolutionary natural-law ideology in Fourier than in Saint-Simon. His starting-point was very much that of Rousseau. Man, he believed, had come out of the hands of nature a good and noble being. The institutions of civilization had brought about his undoing. Greed and avarice were the root of all evil. They had created the existing dichotomies between private morality and commercial and political codes of behaviour, between things preached and ways practised. Morose, ascetic teachings about the evil character of the natural urges were motivated by the avarice and ambition of the greedy and strong, who wished to instil into their victims a sense of sin, and with it humility and readiness to bear privations, perform the dirtiest jobs, and receive the whip. The attempt to stifle natural impulses had the effect of turning the energy contained in them into channels of perversion and aggressiveness.

Such impulses were inflamed by the spectacle of avarice rampant and all-pervasive, in spite of the official ascetic teachings. Fourier may have moralized, may have dreamed of the waters of the oceans turning into lemonade and of lions changed into modern aeroplanes and carrying men over vast distances; but his homilies and dreams are buttressed by a very acute analysis and critique of commercial, if not quite capitalist, civilization. He also analysed history into a succession of social economic stages, and sketched a historical dialectic from which Marx and Engels could – and it seems did – learn something.

Here, however, we are concerned with Fourier's contribution to the problem of organization and freedom. In his view, the state and its laws were instruments of exploitation, and any large centralized state was bound to develop into an engine of tyranny. Fourier therefore held that the state ought to be replaced by a network of small

45   The Suez Canal, officially opened in 1869 (below), was the achievement of Ferdinand de Lesseps, who had been influenced by the teachings of Saint-Simon

46, 47 Right, plan of a 'phalanstère' designed by Charles Fourier (above) and entitled 'The Future'; the first of these was established near Rambouillet in 1838

direct democracies. Each should enjoy full autonomy and be at once a wholly integrated economic unit and a closely-knit political community. In these 'phalanstères' all would be co-partners, everybody would know all the other members (Fourier laid down a maximum of 1800), and decisions would be reached by common consent. By these means men would never be subjected to some anonymous, abstract power above and outside them.

Fourier also tackled the problem of reconciling integration with self-expression. He argued that it was absurd to expect to eliminate love of property, desire to excel, penchant for intrigue or craving for change, let alone sex and gluttony. Such an attempt was sure to engender frustration and anti-social phenomena. And there was no escape from the fact that people had different characteristics and urges of different intensity. Happily, benevolent nature had taken care of that by creating different series of characteristics and passions, like symphonic compositions in which the most discordant elements are united into a meaningful totality. The task was therefore reduced to the art of composing the right groups of characteristics – perfectly integrated partnerships based on the adjustment of human diversities. It followed that the other task was to manipulate the human passions

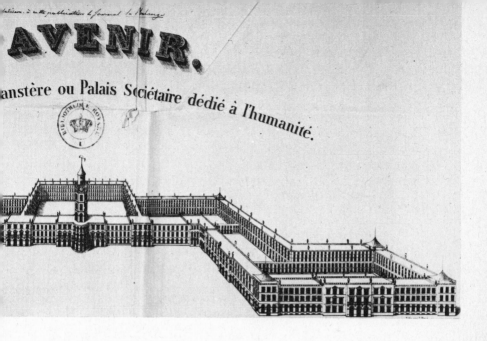

AVENIR.

...anstère ou Palais Sociétaire dédié à l'humanité.

so cleverly that they would become levers of co-operative effort and increased production instead of impediments to collaboration. (This implies an ardent faith in education and environmental influence comparable to Robert Owen's.) To take first the love of property: it would not be abolished or made equal. There would be a secured minimum of private property, but beyond that it would depend on investment, contribution, type of work, degree of fatigue and boredom, and so on, with progressively decreasing dividends. Persons of diverse characteristics joined into one group would stimulate each other, and competition between groups would be strongly encouraged. The paramount aim was to turn labour into a pleasure instead of a curse. In order to obviate the danger of boredom, spells of work would be short and changes in the type of labour frequent. Gangs of children would be set the task of doing the dirty jobs in a spirit of joyous emulation. Finally, industry would be combined with an Arcadian type of agriculture.

This is Fourier's solution to the dilemmas which have plagued our common sense for so long: who will do the disagreeable jobs in a perfectly harmonious society, and what will be the relationship between superiors and inferiors in it?

What was the sum total of socialism in western Europe on the eve of 1848? There was in France a Revolutionary tradition and myth, and a deep-seated, passionate conviction that the Revolution had not really come to an end. It had only been overpowered for a while; indeed it could not come to a stop until it had run its full course and reached the final salvationist station. In that respect a civil war was still going on. Existing governments had no real legitimacy and could not claim allegiance as upholders of objective law and trustees of the people. The devotees of the Revolution professed allegiance to another set of laws, to the legality of the Revolution. The believers in Utopian socialism also felt themselves strangers in the midst of society, waiting as it were for the real thing to start. The first Lyons uprising in 1832, with its revolutionary slogan of 'work or death', was the first major clash between embattled workers and employers (helped by government bayonets), after the employers had gone back upon a formally concluded collective agreement. It was regarded by many at the time as having opened the class war in France, indeed in Europe. Apart from the moribund guild comradeship of the Tour de France, workers had no legal right to organize themselves into unions. Their attempts in that direction were treated as plots against peace and good order. The workers resented the *livret* – the certificate of good conduct issued by the employer – as a downright degradation. In these conditions, no wonder the workers' groups coalesced with the secret political societies, such as the Société des Droits de l'Homme, Société des Familles, Société des Saisons, Phalanges Républicaines, working underground to form, according to police spies (who no doubt exaggerated), compact communist cells on the eve of 1848.

The bourgeois régime was firmly anchored to *laissez-faire* policies, hopefully trusting that things would somehow find their natural level or putting the blame for social difficulties on the improvidence of the workers and the evils inescapable from the human condition. Before 1848 it did nothing by way of social legislation. Public opinion was, however, deeply affected by the shattering findings of men like Buret and Villermé – private individuals, philanthropists,

48   The proletarian Lyons uprising in 1832

doctors and economists, often moved by Christian conscience – who undertook on their own initiative investigations into the conditions of the new industrial proletariat. In the 1840s a proletarian press (*L'Atelier, L'Artisan, L'Echo de Fabrique*) was already expressing the self-awareness of a class which would not allow others to patronize it in a spirit of philanthropy or speak on its behalf as if its members were minors. Also worth mention are the heroic efforts of that remarkable woman, Flora Tristan, to set up a nation-wide trade union organization. Conscious of its major, indeed decisive, contribution to the well-being of the nation, the proletariat would not agree to being supervised by the police. as if they were a group of seasoned criminals. Time was on their side, they loudly declared.

The man epitomizing that evolution was that eternal plotter and prisoner, the grim, tight-lipped high priest of violent *coups*, Auguste Blanqui. No one in the nineteenth-century revolutionary camp preached and practised with such ardour and conviction the idea

73

of the polarization of modern society into the camps of revolution
and counter-revolution. In the struggle between them only force
could decide, force in this case meaning not merely violence, but
conspiracy, plot, surprise, ruse. At his first trial Blanqui indeed asked
the court to treat him as a prisoner of war. This total rejection of
the existing system as evil beyond repair was combined with a
mystical faith that there would be purification and regeneration
once the small vanguard of pure and dedicated revolutionaries had
seized the central artery of power.

The actions of the Orléans government seemed to lend credence
to such visions. Under the impression of a series of outrages culminating in the Fieschi attempt (1835) on the life of the royal family
(which cost eighteen innocent non-royal victims) it adopted the
slogan 'legality will kill us', and issued a series of draconian repressive
laws amounting to a change of régime.

The vast sweep of Saint-Simonian philosophy, the bizarre schemes of Fourier, the economic analysis of Pequeur, the dryasdust writings of the gentle communist bore Cabet, the diffuse but extremely provocative treatises of Proudhon, the pamphlets of Louis Blanc – all this literature underwent a process of percolation and distillation until it reached the working classes. It was absorbed by them in various forms, including the most effective slogan of Proudhon, 'Property is theft', the relevant articles of the 1793 Declaration on the right to work and to social assistance, and the ideas formulated by Louis Blanc under the title *The Organization of Labour*, implying the paramount duty of the state to take over the organization of the nation's economic life. Those workers who imbibed the socialist ideology in one way or another, whatever the distance from the original source, felt sure that the next revolution would be a socialist one. And they had no doubt that such a revolution was imminent.

52  Some six hundred people were injured by the Hussar cavalry in the Peterloo Massacre at Manchester in 1819

THE BRITISH WAY

The total absence of any such genuinely apocalyptic feelings among the British workers is the ultimate reason why social protest never issued in a revolution. This despite the rapidity and extent of the Industrial Revolution, which seemingly made revolution more likely in Britain than France, a country of free peasants, small shopkeepers and independent artisans. Not that there were no revolutionary slogans and rhetoric in the years after 1815 or in the hungry 'forties. But behind the words there was no authentic emotional experience. The British constitution did leave open many safety valves for popular wrath, notwithstanding Peterloo and the articles of the Six Acts. The claim that the law and the courts were mere instruments of the exploiting classes sounded unconvincing even to those who made it, despite miscarriages of justice like the deportation of the 'Tolpuddle martyrs', agricultural labourers who had attempted to set up a union. As the provocation was not extreme, the response could not be so violent. The frame may have bent, but it was not broken. Since there was no violent break, the notion of total change, the idea of planning all anew, never really took hold. This explains the failure of the syndicalist ferment soon after 1830 and of the Chartist movement in the next decade.

The repeal of the Combination Laws in 1824 – the achievement of an indefatigable lobbyist, an outsider without an organization, the tailor Francis Place – was followed not by a demonstration that trade unionism could become a factor of stability, but by evidence that it was an engine of revolution. Organizations with ambitious aims were quickly formed – the General Union of all the Operative Spinners of the United Kingdom in 1829; the General Trade Union of Builders, comprising seven main branches of the trade, in the early 1830s; John Doherty's National Association for the Protection of Labour; and, most ambitious of all, Owen's Grand National Consolidated Trades Union, founded in 1834. All of them sprang not just from the need for mutual aid and for a united front of all labourers, but from a feeling, albeit vague, that justice and history demanded that England should become a Workers' England. This, it was felt, could be achieved through the establishment by the workers themselves of a vast network of workers', producers' and consumers' co-operatives, eventually culminating in a 'Grand National Holiday' – that is, a General Strike – which would destroy the existing state of affairs without the need for violence or political action. The vastness of the scheme, out of all proportion to the possibilities, and even to the motive power behind it, ensured its speedy and total collapse.

53 A membership card issued to the West of Scotland Power Loom Female Weavers Society in 1833, very early in the trade union movement

This failure, coupled with the disappointment caused by the re-formed franchise, and above all by the Poor Law of 1834 (which condemned the unemployed to virtual imprisonment and forced labour in the poor houses), gave rise to Chartism. This was the largest social mass movement in the nineteenth century, and much more in line with British traditions than revolutionary syndicalism. Chartism was made up of diverse and often conflicting social forces and attitudes. The moderate substantial artisans like Lovett believed in self-emancipation through the acquisition of knowledge and skills, and the cultivation of high-minded morality. Tory radicals like Ostler and Stephen hated the hypocrisy of the commercial classes, and the evils engendered by urban industrial civilization. Warm-hearted philanthropists were filled with pity for the toiling suffering masses. There were some, such as the banker Attwood, who believed simultaneously in monetary reform and a wider fran-chise. Political radicals strove for universal suffrage. The demagogue Feargus O'Connor and his followers rejected industrialism out of hand, and preached a back-to-the-land ideology and agrarian populism which ran counter to all the trends of the time. Finally, there were the revolutionary doctrinaires, like Bronterre O'Brien and Harney, who had been deeply influenced by Robespierre and Babeuf, and were in contact with revolutionary émigrés from the Continent. The aim which united them was universal suffrage, but to most of them it was only a means to social revolution. Universal suffrage was sure to give the have-nots a majority. Having acquired political power in a legal manner, they would then carry out legally a social revolution.

There was nothing unconstitutional in the methods the Chartists employed to obtain a parliamentary Act instituting universal suffrage – mass meetings and mass petitions, pamphlets and agitation – so long as they did not turn into riots. The means envisaged as an alternative were of a revolutionary nature. One was the 'Grand National Holiday'. More revolutionary was of course the policy of physical force advocated by the extreme elements. French and American revolutionary influences, and to some extent English con-stitutional tradition, were behind the idea of a Convention: if the

54 'Revolution in the British style': a French lithograph of the Chartist demonstration on Kennington Common in London, 1848

House of Commons refused the demands of the petition, the representative Chartist assembly was to proclaim itself a Convention – a Revolutionary Constituent Assembly – and outlaw the Parliament at Westminster. The Convention, after all, represented the vast majority of the nation, whereas the Members of Parliament were elected by a minority. This is what the Third Estate did in 1789 at Versailles, and what the Soviets were to do in Russia in 1917. As expected, the petition was rejected by Parliament; but instead of revolutionary fervour, bewilderment and confusion overtook the Chartist ranks.

The story of the relations between the government and the Chartists brings into relief the differences between social conflict in England and the Continent. In the first place, the government was extremely careful not to exacerbate feelings. No one was sent to the gallows; Habeas Corpus and freedom of assembly were never suspended; and the participants in the armed Newport uprising – the only serious revolutionary outbreak among the Chartists – were treated without vindictiveness. To give a striking instance, General Napier, the commander of the army sent to face the Chartists, invited the Chartist leaders to inspect his troops. The prudent avoidance of provocation on the part of the government strengthened the deep-seated inhibitions which made the British workers recoil from illegality and arbitrary violence.

Parliamentary tradition and respect for democratic usages paralysed the leadership to such an extent that it decided to hold a referendum on the question of physical force – to be taken almost on the very day when the revolution was supposed to start. One Chartist writer went so far as to suggest importing a few dozen professional revolutionaries from France!

Such inhibitions fragmented the movement and made the Chartists receptive to side-issues – Attwood's paper money ideas, the anti-corn-law agitation, and O'Connor's bizarre, anachronistic land-settlement scheme and crude physical force demagoguery, which alienated the more moderate and responsible elements. The hungry 'forties witnessed the high point, and then the decline of the Chartist movement; even a wave of strikes caused by economic difficulties and amounting almost to a general strike was unable to give it real life. It was significant that the Anti-Corn Law League founded by Cobden and Bright stole the limelight in the middle 'forties. It split the working classes into supporters of the Liberal struggle against the monopoly of landowners and the high price of bread, and anti-Liberals who condemned the League's agitation as a ruse to lower wages by obtaining cheaper bread. The Kennington Common demonstration in the spring of 1848, which filled the propertied classes with such dire forebodings that they mobilized the aged Duke of Wellington to head the forces of order, brought

Chartism to an inglorious end at the very moment when the victory of the revolution in Europe still seemed complete and unshakable.

In the middle of the century the great age of Victorian prosperity set in, and robbed the Chartist issue of its urgency. The middle classes felt deeply secure, and the workers were no longer goaded by unbearable hardships and insults. The period of the New Model began, trade unionism of an empirical, practical type, proving to the employers that the advantages of collective bargaining were more real than the alleged sanctity of individual contracts. Chartism left an afterglow: some heroic memories among the workers; and a certain feeling if not of guilt, at least of discomfort, among the middle classes. Precisely because the Chartists refrained from excesses, a vague conviction developed among the middle classes that the workers had really passed their test of citizenship, and if it was no longer so dangerous to give them a vote, it would be unfair to withhold it from them much longer.

## THE GERMAN INGREDIENT FROM KANT TO MARX

There was nothing in Germany before 1848 to compare with the social unrest across the Channel or the ideological ferment in France. There were already rumblings of discontent in the industrial areas of the Rhineland, and the desperate revolt of the Silesian weavers in the early 1840s was often referred to in the press and in the literature of the day. But political issues still overshadowed the social question, as was inevitable in a country whose industrial revolution had not yet really got going, and in which absolute kings still ruled with the help of the aristocracy. Just about that time, however, the conservative sociologist Lorenz von Stein published his work on the socialist movement in France, bringing socialist ideas to the notice of the German public for the first time. As an intellectual influence it fell on very fertile soil, linking up with a tradition started by none other than the great philosopher Kant.

The earliest exponents of German socialism came from two groups. There were some leftist intellectuals from among the young Hegelians, the 'pure' socialists, who swore by pure theoretical critique and abhorred contamination by contact with practical issues and the compromises and makeshifts inseparable from practical politics. The other group was drawn from radical German artisans in exile in Paris, Brussels and London. Their prototype was the Utopian writer Weitling, and among them were also to be found some intellectuals such as Karl Marx and Friedrich Engels.

*Philosophical preparation*

Kant and his followers are said to have carried out in the sphere of thought a revolution no less significant than the French Revolution, and indeed a revolution which stood for the same things as were brought to the fore by the great upheaval in France. Kant has been compared to Robespierre, Fichte to Babeuf, and Schelling and Hegel to Saint-Simon and Fourier. It was Moses Hess, the other midwife of German socialism, who identified the contribution of each of the three great nations to socialism: France in the field of the revolutionary deed; England in the domain of economics; Germany in the sphere of thought.

Authority, faith, tradition, social milieu: in Kant's philosophy none of these is considered relevant to the man who wishes to know and act rightly. The individual quest must, however, produce results of general validity, and any free resolve as to how to act must be capable of becoming a maxim for all: this was the German formulation of the problem of individual freedom and social cohesion. Kant rejected the reassuring theory of innate ideas implanted in us by God, and enabling our mind to mirror external reality accurately; if that were so, the task of man would be too easy. He refused at the same time to accept the view of Hume and other empiricists that we know nothing but what is perceived by our senses, and since our senses are a manifestly imperfect guide, we can know things only as they appear to us, and not as they really are; our generalized statements about them are therefore no more than inferences from repeated observation and habits of thought. This disconcerting conclusion was at variance with Kant's vision of the dignity of man. Knowledge must neither be made too easy for man, nor denied him as impossible of attainment.

Kant considered man's mind to be not a mirror, but a legislator of nature. Such is its structure that it forces sensations and impressions into rational and objective patterns. It employs for the purpose its innate faculties, as distinct from subjective modes of experience. The faculties are 'intuition' (space and time) and 'understanding' (categories such as causality, reality, substance, unity). There is no way of proving that the latter are able to penetrate into the mystery of the *Ding an sich* (thing in itself). That the world reflected in the mind and the world in itself may not be the same thing does not matter; what does is the possibility of arranging one's picture of the world in such a manner that it has coherence, that it may be communicated to others and that experiments may be repeated at will. In brief, not objective reality but knowledge is the challenge and aim. Knowledge, for Kant, was not a datum but a goal. Here is the measure of man's greatness: he constructs a world by being able to organize his knowledge, and this knowledge proves itself to have objective validity.

55   German caricature of Immanuel Kant with a pot of mustard, 'which he uses with almost every dish'

Kant uses the same point of departure when he considers ethics. Nothing outside man should be allowed to determine his actions as a free rational being making choices. Neither superior external sanctions such as religion, tradition and authority, nor the pull of instinct, sentiment, pity, sympathy, considerations of utility or desire for pleasure, should sway man: his dignity consists in his rational freedom to will things for their own sake because of their objective quality. Any departure from such an attitude and any yielding to extraneous forces is tantamount to a renunciation of freedom: man is an end in himself. But our power of self-direction must be such that the concrete act of self-determination could be adopted by everyone else (this is the famous categorical imperative) so that no one becomes someone else's means or instrument. This is all that one owes to others. In fact any attempt to give more than what is due – from considerations of pity or affection – amounts to an insulting attitude, for it does not treat other human beings as free, self-reliant and ends in themselves, but as a means of indulging one's sentimentality. At the same time, individual actions performed out of obedience to the categorical imperative were certain to set themselves into a harmonious universal pattern.

This is clearly a 'Jacobin' type of morality: all are free and equal, and freely and unanimously will the categorical imperative – virtue. It reflects perhaps a certain social reality, namely of simple relationships, with hardly any hierarchical or collective forms of organization: the small owner, the independent artisan, the petty shopkeeper, each one standing on his own, proud of his unbending rectitude.

Kant was not unaware of the unanswered problems left by this essentially mechanistic and to some extent atomistic approach. Not being able to offer full proof for the answers suggested to him by unresolved mysteries, he contented himself with merely tabulating them as postulates on the epistemological, and antinomies on the ethical plane. Organic structure and purposefulness of nature belonged to the former, the mystery of free will and natural necessity to the latter. Kant's central impulse was less a drive towards absolute objective knowledge than an urge to assert man's freedom, dignity and greatness, and his capacity to form part of a social whole. And this was so in spite of the fact that in his political thought Kant proved himself fully convinced of man's fundamental depravity. Kant's very concept of *Wissenschaft* is charged with accents of an ethical goal.

It is no accident that the most important theoretical achievement of Fichte – Kant's most famous disciple and later his antagonist – is called *Wissenschaftslehre*, although the younger philosopher set out with a much more emphatic reaffirmation of the idea that reality was nothing but a construction of man, and with a passionate refusal to recognize any limits set to the human intellect by the *Ding an sich*.

Fichte envisaged man as a conqueror: the Ego set upon conquering the universe outside itself – the non-Ego – by making it yield its mysteries and fit into the patterns conceived by the mind of man. Every conquest became a spring-board for a new assault. In this respect increase of knowledge, husbandry of natural resources, the rational ordering of society and the state, the emancipation of man from the sway of blind instinct and selfish passion, were all aspects of the march of man. Knowledge and action, intellectual pursuits and ethical progress stemmed from the same impulse and aimed at the same Messianic goal. This was not of course a task for an individual Ego, but for the universal Ego – for mankind across time and space. The more intensely Fichte became aware of the mighty workings of that Ego, the more the individual Ego ceased to matter to him. It was real only in so far as it partook in the infinite endeavour of the universal Ego, in so far as it sublimated its arbitrary self. This was the metaphysical justification of that part of Fichte's political philosophy which found expression in the vision of a closed society and an autarchic near-totalitarian state; in this state the dignity of the individual was secured by having his livelihood guaranteed and his morality enforced by a *Zwingherr* who embodied objective truth and goodness.

While partaking in the collective effort of the universal Ego as a conscious, active and willing participant, the individual Ego inevitably became also a function of that tremendous endeavour which was unfolding itself in stages in time. This was Fichte's contribution towards solution of the subject-object problem, which classical

German philosophy considered as one of its glories, and which was to play such an important part in Marx's thought.

Fichte was not concerned with nature as such – only with man's self-realization through making his impact upon nature, indeed conquering it within himself and outside himself. Nature itself was meaningful only through the imprints which man's presence and work were leaving on it. In their own way Goethe, Schelling and other precursors of evolutionary theory were brought to contemplate nature as history. Nature had evolved from the densest primeval nebula to the most refined specimen of purposeful organization and the highest manifestations of individual consciousness. Man did not stand above and against nature, but was part of its progress. Admittedly his history was the story of the gradual loosening of his ties of dependence upon nature, but even man with the most highly developed consciousness was still part of the general wave of universal history, of a particular stage in the biography of the universal Ego, and indeed in the evolution of the universe. He stood *vis-à-vis* 'things' as a subject and wished to probe and understand them and exercise his activity upon them. But in fact the way he did this was determined by the stage achieved by the world of objects which, though shaped by him, went also to shape him. Here was identity of subject and object. The relationship – it is time to use the expression – was dialectical: the subject made the object, the object made the subject.

Thus the stage was set for Hegel's monumental and revolutionary achievement in system-construction. For millennia European thinking had been dominated by the Platonic and Christian distinction between a world above and a world below; pure ideas and their murky earthly imitations and reflections; theory and practice; perfect heaven and original-sin-ridden earth; reason and senses; spirit and flesh. If not actually a process of progressive degeneration, man's history was significant only in so far as his doings approximated to models of eternal, rational and ethical perfection. Truth was correspondence between actual fact and the abstract objective idea.

Hegel rejected this idea of a world of eternal ideas outside and above human history. The truth of history was in history itself.

56, 57 Fichte (1762–1814), a disciple of Kant, shown in the costume of a Berlin Home Guard, and G. W. F. Hegel

Truth was like a tree unfolding itself gradually and evolving patterns through progressive differentiations and integrations. No sooner had a pattern crystallized than it began to disintegrate under the impact of forces from within which were negating it. Indeed, the full unfolding of the pattern meant that it had brought to fruition all the potentialities of a given stage of evolution, and must therefore die. The force of negation then became the pivot of a higher pattern, into which the earlier one was absorbed as an essential ingredient: the bud, the flower, the leaf, the twig, successively 'die' while giving birth. The history of these mutations was the history of the World Spirit, of necessary consecutive connections which were all rational. At a given stage the Spirit manifested itself in a great diversity of forms, all of which ultimately hung together, and none of which could claim an autonomous existence: not in abstract imaginings, ideas and intentions, but in concrete institutions, laws, achievements – in brief, in embodiments. The world was very mixed and impure: the rational and the irrational, the purposeful and the accidental, the meaningful and the meaningless, the substantial and the contingent, reason and passion, altruism and selfishness, idealism and brute force, dwelt in it together and at the same time. Hegel stated that only the rational was real, and that the real alone was rational; he refused to acknowledge the dichotomies between reason and passion, spirit and matter, and treated the contingent as non-being. Hegel's solution of the problem of these seeming dichotomies was his theory of the cunning of reason. The rational potentiality of man was made truly effective by the coming into action of his powerful passions, selfish and blind as they might seem. Napoleon's dream of self-aggrandizement, for example, egged him on to do things which were ultimately – and in spite of himself – of objective value and great benefit to all mankind. Suffering and destruction were integral to the process: the world had not been created to secure idyllic happiness and individual bliss; birth had always been accompanied by agony. Furthermore, the happy epochs of history had also been its blank pages. The implications of this part of Hegel's thought seem unavoidable. The real/rational triumphs because it is backed by force; it manifests itself through force; in effect force represents – force *is* – the real and rational. Might is right, right is might.

The World Spirit, in Hegel's interpretation, operated through a succession of emergent nations and titanic individuals. Each was, as it were, summoned by its Maker to display in the time assigned to it all its potentialities, and for that time to serve as the distilled essence of the World Spirit and the catalyst of change.

The mixture of nature and spirit, force and freedom, the substantial and the contingent, was most strikingly exemplified in the state in its relationship to society. Society, whether in the form of the family, the corporation, or the voluntary organization, was the sphere of free private pursuits, the object of which was selfish gain. The state, with its apparatus of coercion, gave reality and cohesion to the institutions embodying the World Spirit. And it represented, like (*mutatis mutandis*) Kant's categorical imperative, an end in itself, an objective idea which was not concerned with the advantages it might bring to particular men. Like God, like the pure idea, it exacted disinterested service, absolute loyalty. This became manifest when the supreme test – war – was applied. War was, therefore, the highest proof of the reality of the Spirit, and death the absolute affirmation of the life-force of the idea. As the state – the framework of laws, of the nation's culture and ethos – was the embodiment of the Spirit, obedience to it was the highest manifestation of man's spirituality, and in fighting for his country the aggressive instincts of man were sublimated into fulfilment of a sacred duty.

The question arose: where is the objective nature of the World Spirit to be found, if it is broken up into so many mutations in time, and into so many national spirits at war with each other? For Hegel, the solution of the dichotomy of universality and uniqueness, diversity within unity, lay in the logically inevitable concatenation of the various stages, and in the meaningful structure of each spectrum, notwithstanding the variety of its hues. Will time have no stop, and will mutation follow mutation without end? What element was there in them that was being realized as something of permanent and objective significance? Freedom, Hegel answered. At first the possession of only one man – the Oriental despot – then of some slave-owners, freedom had now become the birthright of every man.

But freedom signified not simply the absence of coercion, but moral freedom, mastery over natural impulse and arbitrary subjectivity; above all, it signified the full comprehension of the workings of the World Spirit through men and things, and the free willing of them. The state, that is, the Prussian state, was such freedom incarnate. In the Prussian state the estates represented society, that is to say, the particular interests of the various sections. It was the king (in spite of, and indeed *because* his birthright was a datum of nature) and the bureaucracy (and army) based on landed property and inheritance – again data of nature – who embodied the impersonal spirituality and idealism of the state.

The Spirit had come to rest because it had achieved full articulation in institutions, whose significance had gained conscious approval.

Force and freedom had thus been brought into full accord. From now on the spirit would be free to roam about only in the realms of religion, philosophy and art – as the Absolute Spirit.

## The young Marx

Hegel had set out to show that there was no history behind history, that history carried its justification within itself, that man, in other words, was self-sufficient and an end in himself. He and his species had not come into the world to serve as a lesson or an example of some truths above and outside them. The logic of their history was the only logic that had any meaning.

This was the point of attack on Hegel by the Left Hegelians, above all by Karl Marx. They accused Hegel of betrayal: he had begun by asserting the self-sufficiency of man, and attempting to prove that it was illegitimate to speak of history other than as the story of man's life, struggles, sufferings, ideas and aspirations; but he had then subordinated history to some World Spirit of which men were made into predicates and manifestations. Their concrete being was denied reality, and reality was granted to them only to the extent that they accorded with or deviated from the self-determinations of the Spirit. Man was asked not to live his own life but to place himself at the service of the World Spirit; in other words, to alienate himself from his own self.

The young Hegelians, especially Feuerbach and Marx, set out to end the self-alienation of man, and to ensure his self-redemption. Any kind of idea put above man, and not flowing directly from the conditions of his concrete existence, produced self-alienation. The supreme example of this was religion. It was not God who had created man, but man who had created God. Out of his misery and sense of nothingness man projected an image of absolute, supernatural perfection, of something that he would have liked to be. The image of an unattainable, absolute perfection confirmed him in the consciousness of his own total unworthiness and hopelessness. He bowed to the perfect Deity and its inscrutable designs, and accepted his fate as a well-deserved punishment. Hence, as part of the endeavour to end this state of affairs, the efforts of such young

58 Karl Marx edited the radical paper, *Die Rheinische Zeitung,* until it was suppressed in 1843. Here he is shown as a Promethean figure, chained to his printing press

Hegelians as Friedrich David Strauss, Bruno Bauer and others to explain the story of the Gospels, and even to deny that Jesus had ever existed. It was, of course, easier to attack religion than the state, but to Marx and those like him the destruction of religion was also a political act – a mortal blow to political authorities which used religion as a prop, and to the Hegelian state as God Incarnate.

For the Hegelian conception of the state as the embodiment of an objective idea, and not as derived from the concrete human situation, was a case of self-alienation of the highest order. Moreover, like the idea of God, it was also a perverted reflection of concrete realities. An image of perfection, standing high above the individual and commanding absolute devotion, divested of concrete social and historical content, the state was a gigantic ruse designed to keep men in subjection and make them accept their lot as God-given.

More concretely, the contemporary constitutional monarchical state of the bourgeoisie had proclaimed all men free and equal, and declared property distinctions irrelevant from the point of view of civil (though hardly, in view of the property-based franchise, of political) rights. It therefore denied the state the right to interfere with property relations.

The most vital sphere of man's existence was thus, as it were, denied relevance, and – more important – emancipated property was thereby given free rein to expand and conquer and subjugate. The purity of the political state was, so to speak, exalted in order that filthy lucre might be pursued without restraint. Might it not be said that property, wishing to throw off all shackles, declared itself irrelevant and raised above itself the perfect political state in order to rivet attention upon that state and distract it from itself? In which case man had been turned from a co-partner in a free state, into a predicate of property, the new Moloch.

Marx further concluded that the modes of production brought to dominance by the Industrial Revolution and capitalism had made unbridled individualism and *laissez-faire* imperative. The very essence of a capitalist economy was endless expansion, without which it would collapse. This was why capitalist property had become a Moloch which condemned not only the propertyless workers, who had been turned into 'hands', to self-alienation but also the capitalists themselves, the masters and factory-owners. Property should *prima facie* have served the bourgeoisie as an instrument of power and a means of free self-expression; but in fact they had become slaves of the monster they had created. This was the imperative of capital accumulation: save and abstain now in order to lay up treasures for the future, and be able to compete with others. In that implacable competition most of the capitalists, not to speak of the middlemen and artisans, would eventually be devoured by a few Leviathans, and would sink into the propertyless multitude. At last, as crisis followed crisis, the few remaining titans would eventually also be crushed under the wheels of a chariot they were no longer able to master.

In opposition to Hegel's vision of a World Spirit reaching its final station in the form of a wholly free humanity, Marx unfolds the vision of a wholly self-alienated species, in which the proletariat is the supreme manifestation of total bondage. In its absolute subjection the proletariat became free from all attachments, because it was denied everything, and therefore attached to nothing. It did not even possess a country of its own. It emerged as pure, unpredicated humanity: neither property-owners nor citizens. Capitalism produced its own grave-digger; its irresistible march created and progressively enlarged the class destined to destroy it: the proletariat. The total opposition of this class to the existing state of affairs was made deadly effective by the vastness of its numbers, its high degree of concentration (brought about by urbanization and the factory system), its utter misery, and finally by the lessons it had learned as the shock troops of every bourgeois revolution against absolutism and feudalism.

Hegel spoke of the unfolding of the World Spirit in men and of their works as vessels. To Marx history consisted in the sum of the concrete forms of human existence, i.e. of man's, or rather society's, struggles to live. The 'pure' socialists, like Hess, Ruge, Grün and the Bauer brothers, pinned all their hopes on critical consciousness grasping the contradictions between outworn forms and the forces straining to break them from within. Under the influence of Cieszkowski and Hess, Marx proclaimed the necessity not merely of comprehending, but of changing reality, or rather of co-operating consciously and actively with the inevitable process of objective change.

Whereas Hegel's World Spirit had come to fruition in the state, i.e. the Prussian state, Marx identified the unfolding of history with the spread of capitalist domination to the outermost confines of the earth, and its consequent confrontation by a world proletariat.

That titanic confrontation would be different from all the class struggles of the past, in which one dominant class was replaced by another. This time it would be the victory not of one class over another, but of humanity itself, and therefore of human freedom. In the past every dominant class had had to resort to the state – its machinery, laws and class morality – to clothe class domination in the garb of objective laws and eternal verities. The victorious proletariat, forming a classless society, would for the first time bring to life essential humanity and true human solidarity. Self-alienation would be replaced by a direct relationship with both fellow-men and nature, in the form of unimpeded reciprocal give-and-take.

The young Marx was thus one of the greatest *exaltés* among the prophets of the Messianic Romantic revolution on the eve of 1848. Like so many of them, he expected the revolution to break out in France. But, unlike some others, he looked to the German proletariat to effect the real break-through once the revolution had begun.

Why the Germans? Because of the tremendous gap between the progress of theory and the backwardness of actual conditions in Germany. This was an abyss to be crossed only by a heroic leap. The proletariat in Germany was still groaning under burdens which no longer oppressed the workers of other countries: landlords and priests, petty tyrannies and military castes. With one terrific heave the German proletariat would shake them all from its back, make a completely fresh start, and bring Reason into its own.

Here we arrive at a point where radical revolutionary universalism touches that other mighty formative force released by the age – nationalism.

59   German cartoon of 1849 showing the 'equal' distribution of the burdens of the state in order to sustain the balance of the crown. The proletariat is crushed by the bourgeoisie, which is in turn burdened by the nobility, according to the ancient law that pressure always comes from above

60
The powers of Europe
attacking the young
French Republic, 1790

SOURCES OF INSPIRATION

The modern nation, and with it modern nationalism as an *idée force*, was born at the moment when, under the inspiration of Rousseau and Sieyès, the representatives of the Third Estate proclaimed themselves a National Assembly. They wished to convey thereby the idea that a nation was an entity, one and indivisible, not to be reconciled with the existence of legally established estates. The nation was, furthermore, master of its own fate, free to determine itself as it saw fit, and owed obedience to no power above or outside it. The bond uniting all was equal citizenship, active partnership in the common weal. The defence and preservation of the liberty of the whole, and of the free and equal status of each within it, was a supreme value. Liberté, République, Patrie became in due course synonymous – as were Jacobin, Revolutionary and patriot – once Republican France was beleaguered by enemies of the Revolution who were also the traditional foes of France. Trees of liberty, *la patrie en danger, levée en masse* and the *tricolore* emerged as the symbols of the new nation and the new nationalism.

It was as yet a purely political conception of nation, drawing its images from the ancient city-republics of Sparta, Athens and Rome. The Revolutionary armies were not fighting for the glory of France eternal or for the increase of her territory and strength. Nor did they consider themselves to be the embodiment of some special French genius and the arm of its mysterious destiny. They fought to make liberty safe at home and to spread its gospel among the nations – in fact to help them to accomplish what the French had done for themselves. This remained true (at least subjectively) even when the lack of revolutionary response on the part of the other nations began to fill French soldiers with pride in their own France - *la grande nation* - and contempt for slave nations that preferred to dwell in darkness

95

and bondage. The logic of centralized republicanism and totalitarian terrorism soon gave rise to a campaign against non-French dialects in the outlying provinces. There arose also the spectre of the foreign plot against the Revolution, hatched by the agents of Pitt and Coburg and embracing all foreigners, among them those parading as cosmopolitan ultra-revolutionaries. None the less, French Revolutionary nationalism remained fundamentally political, democratic and universalist.

At the other end of Europe, and not without close connection with the French Revolution, another type of nationalism took shape, one which might almost be called a Judaic version, that of a conquered, humiliated and oppressed nation dreaming of resurrection: Poland. This proud nation, with a history of well over eight hundred years, had once been a powerful state renowned for its free, well-nigh republican institutions. It had sunk into anarchy as the result of an excess of liberty, and was simply wiped off the map by rapacious neighbours who divided it between them. The national sentiment which emerged under the impact of this unprecedented blow was a trauma, a mystic cult, an obsession, colouring every experience. To the Poles, patriotism could no longer be the loyalty of faithful subjects to their king, nor a sense of partnership in the common weal. It assumed the character of allegiance to an idea, devotion to a ghost. It no longer rested on the soil, it was lodged in men's hearts, as Rousseau had told them it must be, when they sought his advice. After the last partition of Poland, Polish volunteers flocked into northern Italy to form a Polish legion to fight alongside the French army against the common foe; they had a new national anthem: 'Poland is not yet lost. . . . So long as we live'. The severance between territorial government and the subjective sentiment of nationality was something almost incomprehensible to the West, but was destined to be of utmost relevance in central and eastern Europe. It was a man on the far periphery of Europe, and not uninfluenced by Rousseau, who gave tremendous impetus to that phenomenon: Herder.

Herder hated and despised his native Prussia, and had no thought of a political unification of Germany. He defined himself as at once a proud citizen of his adopted city of Riga and a faithful and admiring

61 The Polish revolt of 1830–1

subject of the Empress of Russia, the suzerain of the Hanseatic city. This political syncretism was combined with dedicated service to the supreme values embodied for Herder in the German language and its literature. The subjection to and imitation of French models by German writers and artists filled Herder with indignant anger. The claim that the French patterns were classical models representing the universal criteria of truth, beauty and general perfection was met by him with the statement that his opponents did not know what originality and authenticity of experience and expression were. Anti-classicism and anti-rationalism were thus a facet of the revolt against French cultural preponderance, and possibly, as has been suggested,

62, 63 Johann Gottfried Herder. Opposite, Henry Fuseli, whose visionary work was greatly admired by Herder, painted this illustration for Thomas Gray's poem, *The Bard*

an uprising of the plebeian intelligentsia against the polished society of the French-speaking *salons* of Germany.

Several powers competed for control of the Baltic lands, and different races and civilizations were superimposed there. Herder's experiences in the area drove home to him the lesson that every tribe and people was unfathomably and indestructibly unique – to him a tremendous mystery. Once he began to meditate on this phenomenon, it was only natural for him to wish to probe into the pristine state of each of them, to descend to its primeval, earliest condition, when it was still fully itself and had not yet fallen under the influence of alien models. Hence his passionate, loving interest in these tribes and peoples around him who were still in the folk-loristic, unsophisticated phase – the Latvians and the various other ethnic groups. Herder developed a passion for the unpremeditated immediacy of folk-song, ballad, popular epic, old women's tales, proverbs and sayings. Language emerged as the most significant of all cultural phenomena. There were no two identical languages, and a language was the repository of the unique mentality and heritage of a people.

It was not something consciously and methodically put together, but the result of the workings of primary forces deep in the collective soul. It took many generations to evolve, was never the work of an individual but the fruit of a collective effort begun in remotest antiquity and shrouded in darkness. It was absurd to try to examine the truth or untruth of a language from the point of view of some abstract rational criterion. One took linguistic differences for granted, because one took for granted the differences in experience which they reflected. Yet every language displayed a compelling cohesion, a logic, a reason all of its own. Now might not the same, Herder meditated, be true of the organic growth of peoples and nations? Each nation represented a truth of its own, which was a compound of blood, soil, climate, environment, experience – in brief, race, geography and history. There was no universal criterion by which to judge nations and no absolute model of perfection for them to choose as a yardstick. Language demonstrated that a nation was not what Ernest Renan, in accordance with French Revolutionary tradition, was to call a *plébiscite de tous les jours* – an assembly which men join or secede from according to their conscious conviction – but an organic totality. Men did not create a nation; a nation brought forth men. We do not compile a language like a dictionary: we receive our ideas and feelings from a pre-existing language. The whole was more real, and came before the parts.

So enamoured was Herder of his discovery, so precious to him was the uniqueness of each people, tribe and language, that he condemned the Roman Empire for imposing upon primitive peoples a common language, a universal civilization and institutions; and Christian priest though he was, he condemned medieval Christianity for stifling native creativeness and causing a deep social cultural cleavage between the classes through Catholic Latin universalism. The idea that the strength granted by nature to a people was a measure of its destiny to conquer and become a master of other nations, was alien to Herder. Yet it was inherent in embryonic form in his belief that each nation was a law unto itself, and in his naturalistic, irrational explanation of its uniqueness. The activities of Herder's later life prove that this possibility had not entered his mind. He devoted many years to establishing the correlation between the unity of the history of mankind, and the unique contribution of every tribe, nation and race within that rich pattern.

Herder gave a tremendous stimulus to the nationalism of the Slav peoples. With the exception of the Russians, all of them had by then been subjugated by stronger neighbours – the Germans, Austrians, Hungarians, Russians and Turks. Their development had been arrested at an early stage by foreign rule, and their folk-culture was now in danger of being swamped by the more powerful and richer civilizations of the master races. Under the impact of Herderian Romanticism, scholars, antiquarians, philologists, historians and literati in general embarked upon a feverish activity designed at first to salvage, collect and preserve for posterity, rather than to revive, vestiges of ancient and moribund national traditions. No single generation ever witnessed such a spate of historical dictionaries, learned treatises on grammar, anthologies of old poetry, historical novels, collections of chronicles and sources, and indeed such a flowering of the historical discipline and, of course, patriotic poetry. There was originally no political *arrière pensée* behind these activities of zealous lovers and passionate collectors of the national past. It was the joy of rediscovering a collective identity, and in quite a few cases the expression of an agonized fear that if the work of salvaging were not done at once, the ancient treasures would be lost forever. For the upper classes had already assimilated the culture of the master races, and the pristine purity of the lower orders was already threatened by the disintegrating influences of cosmopolitan urban civilization.

IDÉE FORCE

The quest for national identity assumed political significance when the French Revolutionary example and Herderian teaching coalesced in the Napoleonic era. The Revolution demonstrated the reality of national self-determination by a sovereign people. Napoleon's wars and conquests, his drawing and redrawing of frontiers, sapped the dynastic principle still more. But the nationalism which emerged was of a new type. During the ceaseless minuet of multi-racial armies across Europe the soldiers became intensely aware of national differences. More important, Napoleon's attempt to impose a universal pattern on Europe caused the conquered or menaced nations to respond by identifying their independence with the preservation of their historic way of life and institutions, in short, of their national personality.

The Great Alliance could not have defeated Napoleon if the monarchical principle had been the sole rallying-point. The tables had to be turned upon France, and her own principles had to be invoked and used against her. National armies began to replace mercenary troops. In Germany enthusiastic volunteers played a part in the war of liberation in 1813, and still earlier the instinctive patriotism of the Russian and Spanish peasantries steeped in ignorance, superstition and serfdom developed into a kind of spontaneous *levée en masse*. In 1812 a Prussian general took his courage in both hands, signed a convention with Russian commanders at Taurogi, and changed camps without an authorization from his king, who was

64  A Russian cartoon shows the Tsar in the habit of a Russian peasant holding Napoleon by the scruff of his neck, pointing to him as a wolf in the disguise of a liberator

ПАСТУХЪ И ВОЛКЪ.

65  *The Third of May 1808 at Madrid*, Goya's virulent record of the nocturnal executions of Spanish patriots by Napoleon's soldiers

still technically an ally of Napoleon. In East Prussia junkers and burghers organized resistance against the French on their own, and Stein threatened the princes and princelings of Germany with dethronement if they refused to join the national war of liberation.

No wonder the peacemakers at the Congress of Vienna, assembled to restore the old order, were seized with apprehension. Popular nationalist dynamism threatened to coalesce with revolutionary democratic ideology; both were inimical to dynastic legitimacy. One threatened the integrity of the monarch's possessions, the other the fullness of his authority. In either case the nation – one and indivisible – was the primary and decisive fact.

The monarchist dogma of legitimacy taught that once a country tore itself from the rock of established authority and law, it fell prey to a succession of ever more anarchical ideas and successively worse adventurers and demagogues; finally, tired of chaos and misery, it threw itself into the arms of a usurping tyrant who could maintain himself only by continuous and successful war, offering excitement and plunder. Legitimacy meant a return to the eternal foundations, and the Holy Alliance was to be a European agency to suppress that rebelliousness which had proved itself indivisible, a scourge leaping across all frontiers and disturbing international peace. Respect for the integrity of dynastic possessions was the declared criterion of the great powers at Vienna. In principle the territorial changes made were carried out by mutual consent, and even the wretched King of Saxony, the last of the German princes to remain faithful to Napoleon, was eventually 'persuaded' to cede half his kingdom. The Holy Alliance may at first have been conceived by Alexander I as a pious and earnest resolve by the monarchs to treat their subjects so well that they would never be tempted to revolt. But it required no devilish cleverness on the part of Metternich to turn it into an instrument for preventing or putting down revolutions. Popular upheavals and nationalist rebellion were both part of the same spirit of revolution, which recognized no frontiers. In response to unrest in Italy and Spain the rulers transformed the Holy Alliance into an international organization to suppress revolution everywhere. After the failure of the revolutions of 1820 they took preventive action in the form of universal censorship, concerted spying and general repression, with the stronger power ready to lend a hand to weaker régimes.

Castlereagh and Canning called this arrangement 'a European Areopagus'. A country like England would never join, never countenance, and most certainly never subject itself to such a supranational authority. England had lived and prospered under a régime which had come into being through a revolution. In a parliamentary system the king was not free to dispose of the destinies of his country and to enter upon engagements without the consent of the nation's representatives. And no Englishman relished the idea of Cossacks

66, 67    Tsar Alexander I (left) and Metternich (right)

encamped in Hyde Park, ready to disperse an unruly mob in
Trafalgar Square. Furthermore, it was not the habit of the English to
make arrangements for every possible contingency which might or
might not arise. A sustained, systematic European policy designed to
take the utmost precautions against unrest anywhere was certain to
provoke it, because such a policy was bound to evolve into a
stifling despotism. Animated by panic, it was sure to lose all sense
of proportion and let its full weight bear upon the slightest, often
imaginary, disturbance of public order, even one unconnected with
politics. It was likely in this way to make itself ridiculous and contemptible, and therefore ineffective. And so – British statesmen concluded – each should care for himself, and God would care for all.

If this was not good internationalism, neither was it an apologia for nationalism. Intended as a defence of national sovereignty, the British refusal to co-operate with the Holy Alliance gradually but logically led England to offer direct or indirect support to national movements. Such aid proved highly effective in the case of Latin America, where very important British economic interests were at stake, and suppression from outside could easily be prevented by the British navy in the Atlantic. On the Continent, Britain was neither willing nor able to make her power felt. That is why for nearly fifty years the legitimist powers could frustrate the national aspirations of most of the European peoples, in spite of Palmerston's big-stick blustering.

IDENTITY AND DIVERSITY

The representatives of counter-revolutionary legitimacy were both right and wrong in viewing the various national movements as forming a single whole. The historian sometimes wonders whether to be more impressed by their similarities or by their differences. For instance, it has been pointed out that the growth of urban life was one of the decisive factors in the rise of nationalism in the period after 1815, and this was certainly true of Germany and Italy. Yet in Ireland it was the agrarian problem that was all-important; in Poland and Hungary the gentry played a leading part; and social-economic changes hardly account for the Greek uprising against Turkish suzerainty. It is something of a paradox that a social grievance of burning intensity – that of the Irish – should have evolved into a nationalist fury against the very government which was by any reckoning the most liberal in Europe. No doubt religious oppression made Irish land tenure seem still more odious; and the spectacle of English freedom and prosperity only served to shed a more glaring light on the miseries of the Irish, while enabling Daniel O'Connell to set up a genuine, highly organized and effective mass movement which served as a model to many.

On the European continent the millions of peasants remained unaffected by nationalist sentiments. Serfdom and poverty were more immediately relevant from their point of view than national oppression, and probably everywhere the illiterate peasant still felt himself

THE ABSENTEE Scene Naples  Enter the Ghosts of starved Irish Peasantry !!!

68  Cartoon of an Irish 'absentee' dallying in Naples, and accused by the ghosts of the starving Irish peasantry

to be first and foremost a member of his Church. Continental nationalism was a movement of numerical minorities, above all of the intelligentsia. The aristocracy continued in the majority of cases to be unfriendly. Individual nobles might offer financial assistance to scholars and writers – often tutors to their children – in order to foster a national cultural awakening. They might donate large sums towards the establishment of libraries and institutions of learning, finance the publication of vast collections and, where national self-defence and self-assertion required it, promote co-operative efforts towards economic improvement, like Széchenyi in Hungary. But even those nobles who were liberal enough not to be obsessed by the terrors of Jacobinism, or were bold and generous enough to risk the government's confiscating their goods, were in most cases too hampered by feudal scruples and inhibitions to rise against their kings, whose ancestors had laid the foundations for the greatness of 107 their families. The European *lumpenproletariat* – for example, the *lazzaroni* in Naples – and, for that matter, the nascent industrial proletariat, offered no recruits to the nationalist confraternities. The issues were beyond their ken. To intellectuals, students, and the intelligentsia in general, nationalism was a medium and form of self-expression. It offered a focus for self-identification where the Church had ceased to fulfil this function. There was also something egalitarian about equal membership in a nation, and the liberated nation was envisaged as a country run by men of brains and hearts, not of birth and wealth.

The new modes of production, the revolutionary means of communication, economic expansion and the development of a money economy pointed the way to wider economic and political units, and made the classes representing the new forces receptive to the message of national unification. In the age of railways and rapidly growing trade, internal custom barriers and toll stations were an absurdity in a territorial unit so clearly defined as Italy, and a variety of currencies and weights and measures was an anachronism in a cultural and linguistic entity like Germany. In certain parts of Germany the upper middle class was more likely to support movements of national unity than the petty bourgeoisie, which lived off the small courts and confined its interests to the local market; but in the more advanced states many craftsmen and shopkeepers had been affected by some form of Jacobin ideology.

The logic of their situation, as we shall see, predisposed many Italian and German nationalists to a republican revolutionary solution. But the logic of Hungarian and Polish history pointed in another direction. Their proud and unique heritage of free institutions was the work of a gentry, resting upon the backs of millions of serfs who were to a large extent of another stock. Neither country possessed a native middle class with a national or political tradition. The levelling abstract ideology of democracy and the objective social-economic developments accompanying it threatened the class which had for centuries formed the backbone of the nation – in more than one sense *was* the nation. They constituted a menace to the integrity of a unique historic personality. Emancipation of the serfs carried with it a threat to the very existence of the poorer gentry, while the grant of equal

69 Count Istvan Széchenyi (1791–1860), the Hungarian magnate, helped found an Academy (above) to promote study of the mother-tongue

rights to the very numerous peasants who were of a different stock was sure to undermine the position of the Polish and Hungarian nation in large parts of their historic heritage. Paradoxically, Italy and Germany were eventually united by conservative forces, while the Poles, and for a time also the Hungarians, shone as the knights of revolution. The fact that the three legitimist powers were those which had partitioned Poland made the Poles the supreme test case. As long as the powers remained allied there was hope for neither Poland nor a European revolution, and it was pre-eminently Poland that forced Russia, Austria and Prussia to stay allied.

All the same, in spite of these potential divisions – and in spite of the inherent tendency of any nationalist movement to assert its exclusive particularity – ideology and political alignments combined to invest nationalist movements before 1848 with the features of a universal creed.

The uprising of the Greeks against Turkish rule, the first successful national revolt in the nineteenth century, may well serve as an example of the unique complexity of the problems confronting all the nationalist movements, in spite of their essentially common impulse. The Greek revolt proved conclusively that it was impossible, as the British had claimed, to plan policies against every possible contingency. Well might Metternich complain that the G.H.Q. of the European revolution could not have shown greater cunning than in choosing Greece as the point from which to start a revolutionary conflagration! The magic name of Greece evoked the deepest emotions in men of all shades of opinion. To the enlightened it conjured up immortal memories and visions of future splendours, while even the most *bien pensant* felt unable to treat a revolt of suffering Christians against the unspeakable Turk as simply another act of rebellion against lawful authority. No Tsar, however committed to the policies of monarchical order and suppression of revolution, could remain indifferent when Greek Orthodox bishops were being hanged in their vestments upon the gates of their cathedrals.

Europe knew next to nothing about contemporary Greece; did not know that centuries of Byzantine Christianity, Turkish despotism and isolation from Europe had succeeded in stifling the last vestiges of Classical civilization, and that the modern Greeks were a priest-ridden, quarrelsome nation of small shopkeepers who had long forgotten Sophocles and Phidias, chivalry and civic virtue. Their eyes fixed on the heroes of antiquity, Europeans saw in every Klephtoi chief, usually half-bandit, half-patriot, another Epaminondas or Leonidas. They were shaken to their depths by Byron's death at Missolonghi, by the splendid tableaux of Delacroix and the flamboyant rhymes of Chateaubriand. Western governments were not allowed to sit with folded hands when Turkish and Egyptian forces set out to fulfil the solemn vow of a Turkish sultan, maddened by Greek atrocities, not to leave a single Greek alive. Like the Zionists a hundred years later, the Greeks not only commanded wide sympathy as the descendants of one of the parents of European civilization but were able to make most effective use of their widely

70   Delacroix's painting 'in aid of the Greeks',
*Greece Expiring on the Ruins of Missolonghi*, 1827  ▶

dispersed and often rich and influential communities. In a sense the Greek national liberation movement began not in Greece itself, but among the Greek communities in Vienna, Odessa, St Petersburg, Marseilles and Paris. The early journals, the literary revival, the first conspiratorial groups were all started in these foreign centres, as part of the general European movement, and spread from there to Greece. The first contingent of rebels assembled in Russia and marched in 1821 to the Turkish border, having proclaimed as their leader Ypsilanti, an adjutant of the Tsar of Greek descent. On crossing the border they unexpectedly fell into a trap. The Rumanians would not answer their call to rise against Ottoman rule, and in fact offered their collaboration to the Turkish authorities, thus revealing at an early stage the threat of mortal conflict between the nationalist aspirations of rival national entities.

71  Lord Byron, shown here at the age of 19

72  Otho of Bavaria arriving in Athens in 1832 to occupy the newly erected throne of independent Greece

The Ottoman Empire recognized no nationalities, only religious groups. The Turks were often at a loss to account for the differences among the ethnic or linguistic groups professing the Greek Orthodox religion. The Greeks were the leading group among them, and the Greek Orthodox Patriarch in Constantinople, invariably a Greek, was the head of all the Christians in the Empire. Since religion and culture were indistinguishable in that part of the world, and the native cultures of the other races – Rumanians, Bulgarians and other South Slavs – were still in their most rudimentary stage, there was a natural inclination on the part of both Turks and Greeks to lump all Christians together as in some way Greeks. Greeks had indeed served for generations as dragomans, or provincial governors, and in Moldavia and Wallachia as hereditary hospodars on behalf of the Sultan. The Greek rebels took it for granted that at the first call the Rumanians and others would spring to arms to help the cause of the Greeks and

113

– in the Greek view – of general emancipation. But the Rumanians would not budge. On the contrary, they helped the Turks to round up the Greek fugitives after their terrible defeat. The notion of an international revolutionary confraternity embracing all rebels against the principle of dynastic legitimacy was disproved. Public opinion was, therefore, able to force the hands of governments, above all the British and French – in spite of the fact that Britain had every reason to fear the dismemberment of the Ottoman Empire and a Russian protectorate over a weak Greek state, and that France had no important interests in the Balkan peninsula. Britain was the first to recognize the Greek insurgents as a belligerent party, on the somewhat specious ground that such recognition would stop Greek acts of piracy. A British admiral was in command of the combined navies of the Christian powers which at Navarino annihilated – without a declaration of war – the Turko-Egyptian fleet carrying troops to administer the final *coup de grâce* to the Greek rebels. The Duke of Wellington's government was intensely chagrined by this 'most untoward incident'. Tsar Alexander I had remained inactive, torn between legitimism and his duties as the lay head of the Greek Orthodox Christians in Europe. His successor, Nicholas I, was not much bothered by either commitment, but wanted very much to extend his rule over the Danubian provinces. As in many similar situations in the future, power politics gave a helping hand to a movement of national liberation and served as the lever of a humanitarian cause. It was left to France to act on behalf of Europe as a kind of United Nations force – and not as an expeditionary force of the Holy Alliance, as she had done in Spain a few years earlier – and to supervise the establishment of Greek liberty, after the Russians had forced Turkey to her knees. Exhausted, their country in ruins, with continuing civil strife accompanied by murder and pillage as well as the assassination of the first President, Capo d'Istria, former counsellor to Tsar Alexander I, the free Greeks gave Europe a foretaste of the disillusionment that in the future was all too often to follow the exalted hopes engendered by a struggle for national liberation. It was no crown of roses that the powers offered Otho of Bavaria in 1832.

73　*The People of Rome*, a lithograph of 1823

Italian nationalism contained many of the features of the Greek movement, while at the same time possessing all the characteristics necessary to make it the ideal type of a nationalist ideology in the first half of the nineteenth century. No less than Greece, Italy embodied a tremendous myth of universal appeal. But unlike Greece, the Byzantine phase of which western Europe did not care to remember, Italy represented several myths: the myth of the Roman Republic, the myth of the Empire, the myth of the papacy, the myth of the medieval free city-states, and of the Renaissance. While the Byzantine myth was calculated to be exploited by the Tsars of Russia, but was irrelevant to other countries of Europe, the myth of the Roman papacy was of intense significance to hundreds of millions of men, as well as to some of the greatest powers of the age. Furthermore, the Papal State constituted a wedge between the northern and southern parts of the Italian peninsula. Thus, paradoxically, a territory which seemed to have been intended by nature to constitute an entity from the racial, linguistic and cultural (though not from the social-economic) point of view, and was inhabited by one of the most homogeneous populations in Europe, was claimed by mankind as a whole. Moreover, its inhabitants themselves were not at all eager to regard their country and history as being an exclusive concern of their own. They were intensely and proudly anxious to be regarded as carrying out a mission on behalf of mankind. The semi-religious Italian version of nationalism – above all in the person and teachings of Mazzini – was consciously a replica of the papal myth.

Objective realities gave force to these feelings. Against the logic of a single nation inhabiting a sharply contoured geographical unit stood the unreason of territorial-political divisions: Lombardy and Venice under direct Austrian rule, a succession of small states all, with the exception of Piedmont, ruled by foreign dynasties, and finally the papal domain. Italy could be united only by the deposition of the dynasties, or at least by the recognition of the supremacy of the one and indivisible nation, which might or might not deign to leave the princes on the thrones of the constituent parts of a federal Italy. In this respect democratic anti-monarchism and nationalism were inseparable. Furthermore, with the exception of the national dynasty in Piedmont, all the rulers of Italy were closely related to the House of Habsburg. The Holy Alliance had appointed that ancient dynasty guardian of legitimacy in Italy. It ruled over the most massive bloc of Catholic populations in Europe, and had served for centuries as the secular arm of the papacy against Protestants and Turks.

To be an Italian nationalist, therefore, meant to be an anti-papal, anti-Habsburg, anti-legitimist republican, and thus to be alongside the Poles in the vanguard of all the forces in Europe ranged against the Holy Alliance. Mazzini proclaimed the nineteenth century the age of the arrival of the nations, just as the socialists heralded it as the age of the arrival of the proletariat. All history was a preparation for that solemn fulfilment. The World Spirit, unfolding itself across time and employing at each stage a different vehicle, had now embodied itself in the nation. It had done so in earlier ages in the Roman Empire and later in the Roman papacy; and just as they had had their seat in Rome, so the Rome of the future, *Roma Terza*, would guide the destinies of the nations.

The nation was a confraternity, sharing the same destiny, fulfilling a definite mission, welded into one by intense sentiments of love, devotion and pride. God and the people: Providence was hovering over the nation like the God of the Hosts over His Chosen People, Israel; and there was a kind of covenant between the people and the

Almighty. The life of the people was a life of service, and its highest manifestation was the strenuous fulfilment of duty and self-sacrifice. The individual was to be guided not by personal liberty and self-interest, but by the ardent wish to play the part which the nation, bent upon carrying out its mission, had assigned to him. He was to do this not in the spirit of blind subjection to higher authority or external compulsion, but through conscious and strenuous yet freely willed self-identification with the destiny of the nation, as an equal among equals. In brief, the nation was a holy people, a nation of priests, in contrast to the Catholic division into a superior teaching hierarchy and the mass of simple, passive believers.

In contrast again to the Catholic Church, the national confraternity would be based upon the unity of life, and would reject all distinctions between theory and practice, Heaven and earth, Church and State, social and individual ethics. Service to the community in a spirit of undivided, enthusiastic loyalty was the highest form of worship, because it meant fulfilling the will of God, in other words the decrees of History. The dilemma of tension between the individual and the collectivity was resolved by the Saint-Simonist emphasis placed upon the dynamic character of collective existence – that of a permanent preparation for some break-through, in which the highest degree of integration ensured the fullest measure of individual self-expression. Literature, the arts, ideas, the whole life of the spirit was judged from the point of view of its social-religious function in harmonizing the sentiments of the individual with the life and endeavours of the whole.

This conception of the nation enabled Mazzini to deny the claims of France to be the leader of the European revolution. France had completed her mission in the French Revolution by liberating the individual from the shackles of priestly and kingly despotism. But that high mission was essentially a negative one of protest and destruction. It abolished outworn forces and set man free. But it offered no new principle of integration. That was provided by the idea of the nation, represented by Italy.

The nation, or people, was a social category, in that it signified the arrival of the masses, of equality instead of privilege, of a kind of puritan asceticism as against self-indulgence by selfish individuals pursuing nothing but gain and pleasure. The Mazzinian concept of the nation was thus charged with accents of social radicalism. But it was not compatible with socialist insistence on modes of production as the motive power of historic change, and certainly not with the ensuing concept of class war as the underlying reality in the life of societies. No nationalist theory can afford to consider the nation as anything less than the primary fact of history and a brotherhood in which there is no place for selfish privilege or cosmopolitan anarchism. Mazzini condemned laissez-faire because the national good came before self-enrichment; but he was also bitterly opposed to communism, because an exclusive emphasis upon centralized direction of the economy left no room for idealism and self-sacrifice, and none for the uniqueness of the nation and the national spirit. The Italian workers would not be free so long as the Italian nation was in bondage, Mazzini claimed; by contrast Marx told the Germans that Germany would not become free until the German proletariat had emancipated itself.

The national aspirations of subjugated and divided peoples embodied, in the eyes of Mazzini, the quintessence and the nobility of the age. These peoples formed a single religious movement locked in struggle with the forces of oppression, which embodied all that was evil and foredoomed. A national movement must not make compromises or attempt to exploit the shifting alignments of the powers. Any form of contact with oppressors of other nations would be to betray the sacred cause of national liberation, which was one and indivisible. The peoples were to meet the encamped forces of the kings in one frontal assault. Mazzini spent many busy years of his exile, after his dismal failure to lead a national liberation force from Switzerland into Italy, in setting up (largely on paper) general staffs for insurrectionary Young Italy, Young Germany, Young Poland, etc., under a no less imaginary General Headquarters of the imminent European revolution.

This belief in the common cause of peoples striving for national self-determination was a fundamental tenet of Mazzini's. He sincerely believed that the principle of nationalities was the essence of morality,

74 'Psychographic' portrait of Mazzini. The letters (a), (b) and (c) denote 'divine wisdom', 'patriotism' and 'liberality'

and was furthermore an eminently practical basis for redrawing the map of Europe. He never conceived of the nation as a law unto itself, not bound by a universal natural law, and was far from considering expansionist, dynamic vitality as a sign of worth and merit. Nevertheless, the national mission, the nation as an all-embracing religious confraternity, dreams of a restored Mediterranean Roman Empire – all to be found in Mazzini's pages – could·in other minds become the foundations of an aggressive and exclusive nationalism, and indeed totalitarianism.

The dilemma of nationalism and universalism was fundamental in another theory of Italian nationalism, that of Gioberti. For all its momentary popularity, it was doomed from the start. There was really no possibility that the Pope, as both the head of the universal Church and a ruler of central Italy, could become the leader of a united federal Italy. Just as there is a limit to the universalism of any national movement, there is a definite limit to the ability of the papacy to identify itself with a nationalist movement (let alone head it) or to make concessions to liberalism.

Massimo d'Azeglio and other writers and politicians quite consciously eschewed appeals to universalism, once they reached the realistic conclusion that the royal House of Piedmont was destined to take the initiative in liberating Italy. Piedmont had no claim to represent a historic tradition of universal significance; it would have to unite the various states under its rule by opportunism – by making alliances and taking advantage of quarrels between the powers as they arose, without reference to moral issues. The opportunist approach thus replaced revolutionary resolve and Messianic expectation of an abrupt and universal change. Piedmont had to be made a worth-while ally through a systematic accumulation of economic assets and the building up of military strength. Greater national cohesion was to be achieved by promoting endeavours which called for co-operation and created important common interests – industrialization, road and railway building, banking institutions, agricultural improvement. There were other important developments. A flourishing literature – Manzoni's *I Promessi Sposi*, Leopardi's poetry, the moving descriptions of Italian patriots in Austrian prisons; the martydom of idealistic youths who heeded the teachings

75, 76 Schiller (left) and Goethe (seen right in the portrait painted by Tischbein in the Campagna)

of the exiled prophet Mazzini; the close ties forged between scholars and scientists at the all-Italian congresses – all these contributed towards the deepening of a sense of the unity of the Italian people across the frontiers dividing them.

For a long time many Germans justified and even glorified German disunity with the claim that the destiny of the Germans was to be the Greeks of the modern world – a nation composed of many states but constituting a single glorious civilization. Was not the great variety of political forms, even the struggles between the states, the secret of Greek richness and vitality in all fields?

To the very end of the eighteenth century, and indeed beyond it, the finest spirits of Germany took pride in being free of any feelings of exclusive German nationalism, to the point of ridiculing such inbred sentiments. They considered themselves the spokesmen of humanity writing in the German language. According to Schiller it was the mark of a true German not to be solely and exclusively German, and not to be obsessed by politics, but to live the life of the

spirit. The historic myth of Germany was not that of a national state, but of the Roman Empire of the German Nation. As such it embodied the tradition of a universal empire whose values, obligations and interests transcended that of territorial Germany. Theoretically at least, the Germans were not the sole and undisputed sovereigns of that empire: if in some vague way other nations were under its suzerainty, they were also, in however nebulous and undefined a way, entitled to have a say in its destinies. In theory, a French king or a Spanish prince or anyone else could submit himself as candidate for the imperial throne. It was not as Germans that the Habsburgs of Austria came into semi-hereditary possession of the imperial crown. They would certainly not have identified themselves as such. As late as the early nineteenth century, even so ardent a patriot and keen a reformer as Stein was prepared to call on Britain and other states to guarantee the integrity of the German empire and to share in the control of its destinies.

One stumbling-block on the way to unity was of course the division of Germany into Catholics and Protestants. The other was the special position occupied by the two most powerful components of the German empire, Austria and Prussia, which had spread their dominion over non-German territories, and had for generations conducted policies which had nothing to do with authentic German interests.

There were other important factors which made the Germans an apolitical nation. Most of the little states were so small and altogether so ludicrous – with their lilliputian armies, their aping of Versailles and their parish-pump absolutism – that they could hardly inspire pride or even respect in the more courageous and stronger spirits, or claim their talents for the running of the government. Hence political alienation.

If politics and patriotism could not claim the devotion and energies of the educated classes, things of the spirit could and did. This was the reason for the baffling contrast between the parochial character of a large part of German political and economic life, and the wealth, breadth and daring of their spiritual preoccupations and the universality of their intellectual interests. This dichotomy also had deep spiritual roots. Luther bequeathed to the German people the Pauline tradition, which puts great emphasis upon the inner light and the life of the spirit. He is free who feels inwardly redeemed and free, even if he is a slave in the world; and a king or magnate in the world remains a slave if he is in bondage in his heart. While leading to introspection and thus calculated to give depth and intensity to the inner self – as it did in the case of pietism – this is a doctrine which, by deprecating the external world as irrelevant, may end by sanctioning it as it is, and bowing to the evil and tyranny in it.

Just at the moment when a spiritual-cultural renaissance of extraordinary diversity and splendour was placing the German nation in the forefront of civilization the political disintegration of Germany became complete. In the wars between Frederick the Great and Austria, the last shred of a German community of interests had been torn to pieces. Then came the French Revolution, which for a while won the heart of every enlightened person in Germany, deepening the alienation of the intellectuals from their own states and governments. It is enough to quote only one case, that of Fichte, the future prophet of German nationalism. In the first years of the French Revolution Fichte was praying for the triumph of Revolutionary France over the troops of the German princes, and soliciting the post of a French professor at the University of Strasbourg in order to be able to win German youth over to the ideals of the French Revolution. He professed to feel a total stranger in his country of birth. The fatherland of the enlightened man was the country which at a given moment was in the vanguard of progress. The face of the free man was turned towards the light of the sun; and France was at that moment humanity's column of fire. In Germany, Fichte claimed, the current of events was such that within a few years not a free thought would be left.

The Napoleonic conquest of Germany, far from upsetting the German intellectuals, rather evoked deep admiration for the superman, the new Alexander, who to Hegel was the World Spirit on horseback. The rulers of Germany fell over each other to submit humbly to the French conqueror, in the hope of winning some morsel from him. Napoleon brought about the final demise of the

Roman Empire of the German Nation, and turned the German states into a pack of cards to be shuffled and reshuffled at will. In the process, the Germans revealed an astonishing characterlessness, not the much-vaunted German attachment to tradition and Teutonic loyalty to principle. This was most strikingly revealed in the total collapse of Prussia in 1806–7, when fortress after fortress opened its gates without a shot, and all effective resistance to the invader collapsed. When the cup seemed full, a far-reaching revulsion of feeling set in in Germany, above all in Prussia, which partly fed on developments which will be discussed in the section on Romanticism.

At an earlier stage, the convulsions of the French Revolution, culminating in terrorist dictatorship and internecine massacres, soon frightened many of its German admirers. In their eyes the French had proved that they did not know what freedom – that is to say, moral freedom – was. 'Liberté' had become an opportunity and instrument for self-willed arbitrariness and the rule of brute force, shocking to German moral seriousness, deep piety, love of order, respect for law.

Under the influence of Burke, French abstract levelling rationalism came to be regarded as shallow and fundamentally untrue, since it ignored the authenticity of race, national tradition, *Volksgeist*, slow organic growth. Its irreverent and ignorant presumption to impose uniform patterns by force did violence to the peculiar individuality of historic phenomena. Far from being a promise of liberty, therefore, it was a threat to genuine, concrete freedom embodied in custom, habit, cherished traditions and idiosyncrasies.

The feudal state began to be idealized as the model for organic relationships, in contrast to the mechanical contrivances of the rationalist theoreticians and legislators. The state as such was then rather surprisingly accorded – notably by Adam Müller – supreme reality, as being logically prior to all its component parts. It was hallowed as an indivisible entity and as the source of all values and morality, and indeed as a work of art. Before long the uniqueness of the German tradition was held to have the kind of universal significance that the French claimed for their ideology of natural law and the rights of man.

77 Professor Heinrich Steffens, the German philosopher and physicist, calling on the people of Breslau to resist Napoleon in 1813

The anti-French nationalists made much of the myth of Arminius, the Germanic hero who beat back the Roman invaders and thus saved the German tribes. Tacitus' *Germania* was of great use in this. Whether the morose Roman historian really believed in his idealized picture of the good, noble Germans or wished to use it to bring into relief the vices of contemporary Roman society, the fact remains that for centuries German schoolboys studied *Germania* as a genuine portrait of their ancestors. It is hardly surprising that they showed themselves so receptive to an exclusive nationalism, and eventually to racialism. The myth received powerful scholarly backing and confirmation from the highly respectable 'historical' school of jurists founded by Savigny. It rejected the idea of a universal source of law and justice and a universal sanction for laws – in other words natural law – and claimed the national spirit and the unique national history to be the source of all laws, and of the idea of justice prevailing in any nation.

These ideas contained implications which were by no means welcome to conservative legitimists. They invoked the mysterious unfathomable quantity of *Volkstum*, which overrode the principle of authority vested by God or history in some person or dynasty. They substituted for the loyalty of the subject to the dynasty or the chivalrous allegiance of retainers to their lord a *Volksgeist* which could embody itself in a variety of forms and institutions. All that mattered was that they should express the authentic spirit and interest of the national community; and when they ceased to do so, they should be rejected. Equally unacceptable to conservatives was the further implication that there could be no other judge of the fitness of institutions than the people itself. Admittedly it was unclear how the people's judgment could be expressed; but the very concept of *Volkstum* had a certain plebeian ring, or at least could be made to refer to those layers of society which in their unsophisticated simplicity were closer to the roots of national history. All the same, in the national Pantheon there was room for a Barbarossa and a Luther, an Arminius and a Great Elector, Teutonic Knight and Meistersinger, the Nibelungen and burghers, good old peasant stock and the poetry of Kleist.

78, 79  Cultural nationalism. Peasant costume in Baden (left) and Russian peasants dancing

80, 81, 82 Poets of patriotism. Achim von Arnim, collector of folk-songs; Theodore Körner, composer of patriotic songs and poems, who died in the German war of liberation; Ernst Moritz Arndt, whose patriotic anti-Napoleon songs gained wide popularity

Moritz Arndt, Körner, Father Jahn, Arnim were the prophets of this type of *völkisch* patriotism – replete with patriotic poetry and songs, nationalist symbolism, the cult of ancient German customs, national dress and national folk-ways, linguistic purism and medieval duelling, strenuous living, heavy drinking and exhibitionist rowdyism designed to intimidate and inhibit opponents, especially Jews.

The *völkisch* ideology was a direct denial of all universalism. It was at first reinforced by ideas which had their roots in natural law philosophy, but later began to veer away in the opposite direction.

Fichte's flaming addresses to the German nation contain a violent condemnation of the characterlessness and cowardly selfishness displayed by the Germans under the blows administered by Napoleon, and a stirring call for a return to the true, authentic German self. On closer scrutiny this turns out to be an apotheosis of deep human spirituality and strength of character, as opposed to a political listlessness and aimless drift. Fichte does not refer to any glorious martial traditions or to deeds of conquest in the German past. In fact, he says in so many words that the Germans, being a mature nation of spiritual depth, would not stoop so low as to compete with other

127

nations – the British, the French, the Spaniards – in the subjugation of other races, in the exploitation of primitive tribes or in the scramble for wealth and power. Their destiny was to serve as an example of devotion to values that are the pride of the human race, to create and uphold them with a fierce, self-denying tenacity.

By being truly German Fichte also meant being authentically creative – that is, in obedience to a primary irresistible impulse, and not by way of deliberate contrivance. The Germans were *the* creative, *the* original race among the European nations, the *Urvolk*, because they were the only great nation in Europe to have kept their original language. The British, French, Italians and Spaniards had taken over a language from another people and turned it into a kind of jargon; as imitators they lacked immediacy and originality, and could at best produce variations on the original creative achievements of others. In this rhapsody on the *Urvolk* and *Ursprache* Fichte took leave of his earlier rationalist and mechanistic modes of thought. The *Ursprache* was something unique that was mysteriously there, a datum of nature. This contains the pregnant suggestion that spiritual content is predetermined by some natural, ineluctable forces.

The peacemakers at Vienna, as we have seen, had no use for any *Volkstum* ideology. The governments of the different German states invoked local, not national, traditions to buttress the principle of dynastic legitimacy, and the German Bund created in 1815 was to be a league of German states, and not the political-juridical framework of a united German nation.

Such a setback to the hopes of national unity at the hands of the guardians of the monarchical order was calculated to revive liberal and even radical opposition. The issue of revolution became central. As in the case of Italy, abstract logic pointed to a republic. There was ultimately no middle position between dynastic legitimacy and popular sovereignty. Once legitimacy was denied on constitutional grounds, the right of separate states to exist at all would inevitably be rejected on national grounds. If there was a single German nation with a right to determine its fate, and if no king had a divine right to dispose of the destinies of his subjects, the constitutional liberal became a nationalist, and the nationalist was driven to become a democratic republican. A unified national republic was clearly impossible without the victory of a spontaneous general revolution, or, failing that, without the imposition of the revolutionary ideology on the recalcitrant and the indifferent. In either case it was hardly feasible without an external war against those, above all Tsarist Russia, who were sure not to accept a powerful Red republic in the heart of Europe. In which case there was no escape from a total European revolution. That is why radical revolutionaries like Marx became for a while ardent nationalists. A republican revolution to establish German unity would be driven to take extreme terrorist measures against the dynasties, the aristocracy, the officer corps, the Church, and large parts of the bourgeoisie. The same broom would sweep away all the cobwebs left by an absurd past and an oppressive social order, and the new Germany would carry revolution across Europe. Such were the voices heard at the famous Hambacher Fest in 1832.

The Red spectre was enough to make many patriotic liberals pause and think. It led men influenced by British constitutional practice and general empiricism, as well as writers who drew their inspiration from the French liberal ideas of the Doctrinaires and Benjamin Constant, to consider the possibility of a federal solution which would avoid a revolutionary destruction of thrones. In order to obviate the vexed question of sovereignty and dispel the spectre of revolutionary coercion by force, Rotteck and Welcker developed the idea of the *Rechtsstaat*. Modifying somewhat the French Doctrinaire theory of the sovereignty of reason, they argued that sovereignty resides neither in the king nor in the people, but in the law.

Liberal German nationalism was thus faced with a difficult task: to avoid a revolutionary destruction of thrones and existing states, and at the same time to persuade the existing states, if not to efface themselves, at least to subordinate themselves voluntarily to an all-German structure. The more powerful, better-formed, and more highly integrated the individual German state was, the more formidable it was as an obstacle to German unity. An arrangement which left the individual states in existence was possible only under the aegis of Austria or Prussia, the only two German states with the necessary power and standing to impose unification.

Austria's supremacy was more acceptable in the eyes of the Catholics, since it would have prevented the hegemony of northern, mainly Prussian Protestantism. It was also more acceptable to the southern states, because the less stringent traditions and the looser form of the Habsburg empire promised a large degree of autonomy to each of the component parts of a future federation. Furthermore, the very name of Habsburg meant linking up with a long unbroken tradition. Unfortunately, it also stood for a direct denial of the national principle. It was hardly possible to ask the ancient dynasty to divest itself of its vast non-German heritage in order to head a united state of Germans. It was equally difficult to imagine a political structure in which the Germans (including Austrian Germans) constituted a modern nation-state under Habsburg rule based upon the national principle, while the non-German Habsburg domains retained their character of hereditary dynastic possessions resting upon divine right and feudal law.

The Habsburgs, a most tenacious dynasty, throve on the vitality of the feudal-dynastic principle and on the contradictions and conflicts engendered by the principle of nationalities. The aristocracy of the Danubian empire was truly cosmopolitan, and its allegiance to the dynasty outweighed any loyalty to its particular race. Indeed, some of its members would have been hard put to it to define their race, for many of the nobility were descendants of Spanish, Scottish, Irish, Italian, Dutch and other Catholic warriors and adventurers who had come to Central Europe to help the Habsburg cause during the Thirty Years War in the seventeenth century. They had fought as volunteers or mercenaries and had been rewarded by the Habsburgs with lands forfeited by rebel Protestant gentry, especially in Bohemia and Moravia. The Catholic Church was the other pillar of the Austrian idea. Its immense influence upon the peasant masses was directed towards instilling into them a spirit of unquestioned semi-religious loyalty to the emperor. And on occasion the imperial government was Machiavellian enough to unleash the faithful peasants against the gentry and the bourgeoisie (as it did in Galicia in 1846) in order to silence opponents and inhibit the upper and middle classes from playing with rebellion.

83  Francis I (until 1806
Francis II of the Holy
Roman Empire),
denounced by the liberals
as a tyrant, but popular
amongst his people

It was a deliberate policy on the part of the Habsburgs to keep the nationalities together (as Francis II disarmingly confessed) by inciting them against each other – by stationing Croat troops in Italy and Hungarian dragoons in Bohemia, by upholding Ukrainian peasants against Polish gentry and supporting Rumanians against Magyars in Transylvania. The Austrian government was not as yet worried by the cultural and literary nationalism of such nationalities as the Czechs, Croats, Ukrainians and Rumanians, for its standard-bearers were a small group, the intelligentsia. The nationality issue reached its acute stage only later in the century. So long as Austria remained a mainly agricultural country with little social mobility, its races, so to speak, lived side by side. It was when industrialization drove or attracted the peasant masses into towns, forcing them to face employers and foremen or skilled workers of different speech

131

and race, that national self-awareness and nationalist animosities really became inflamed. Before 1848 the most urbanized part of the empire was the German-speaking provinces, and their inhabitants were of course the dominant element in the state. So long as their hegemony over the other races was unquestioned, they felt no pull towards a united Germany. It was at a later date, when the rise of the Slavs and (still more important) universal suffrage began to threaten the privileged position of the Germans – a numerical minority but an economic and cultural *élite* accustomed to rule – that the Habsburg empire entered upon its real crisis.

With Austria still powerful and dynastically-minded, and Prussia intensely conscious of her unique past and achievement, the vague national aspirations of the liberal intelligentsia seemed to lack an effective instrument. This was provided at an early date from another quarter and for quite different motives.

The *Zollverein*, that mighty lever of German unification, started as an internal Prussian measure, designed to weld her widely dispersed provinces into a single economic unit. Abolition of internal tolls and customs meant loss of revenue, and forced the Prussian government to seek compensation in higher external tariffs. The victims of this policy, the smaller buffer states, had no choice but to seek admission into the new customs union. As a result, most of Germany had by 1848 become a highly effective customs union.

84   A satire on German customs
before the *Zollverein*

Although the original motives for this development were purely fiscal, it was soon reinterpreted as a semi-conscious move of the German genius towards the fulfilment of Germany's destiny. It received a philosophical foundation directly opposed to the most cherished dogmas of British economic liberalism: List's *Das nationale System der politischen Ökonomie* (1841) was a defiant repudiation of Adam Smith's teachings about the individual's natural right to seek the highest reward for his skill and labour and about the primacy of economics over politics. Freedom of trade, claimed List, suited only powerful nations. In a nation struggling for an independent status and attempting to build up its economy the individual must be subordinated to the collectivity. England, with her near-monopolistic position as the leading industrial nation, could afford *laissez-faire* at home and was naturally interested in free trade, since she could thereby swamp every market and prevent the rise of competing industries in weaker states. These had therefore no choice but to raise protective tariffs. List also attacked Smith's views by arguing that if political power was a function of economic strength, economic power was also conditional upon political strength: a nation victorious in the field of battle dictated economic terms to the vanquished. The well-being of the individual was thus a function of the powerful position of the nation, and a nation's strength was the outcome of individual self-sacrifice. List's vision of 'a common German fatherland'

85  Caricature of the *Zollverein* liberating Germany from the bonds of 'Liverpool' and 'Manchester'

held out the possibility of a future united Germany as the focus of a Middle European economic unit stretching from the Baltic to the Black Sea, and from the Adriatic to the North Sea; German colonists would be planted in the neighbouring states of the European south-east, directing its energies towards the oceans and intercontinental trade.

On the purely political plane an incident occurred in 1840 which had a traumatic effect on the Germans. The government of Thiers, thwarted in its imperialist ambitions in the Middle East, and entirely isolated by the concert of powers which brought about the downfall of Mehemet Ali, decided to put pressure on another front. It unchained an agitation for the 'natural frontiers' of France in order to gratify traditionalists extolling the greatness of Richelieu, as well as the upholders of the glory of the Grande Armée, who in a way comprehensible only to themselves thought they could combine the patriotic claim to natural frontiers with revolutionary universalism. The German reaction was a wave of nationalist hysteria. The *Wacht am Rhein*, the famous patriotic song, was composed at this time. Nationalist fervour gripped all classes, acting as an all-German nationalist cement, and at the same time bringing into strong relief the position of Prussia as the spearhead of the German nation.

86   The Rhine crisis of 1840. A caricature contrasts the calm of the French on the left bank, and the ineffectual hysteria of the Germans on the right

# V ROMANTICISM

The enthusiasms and passions, the flights of thought and of idealism, the theories, aspirations and illusions, however contradictory they appear, and of course the artistic endeavours of the age – may all be viewed as the refractions of one great light, that of Romanticism. It was that all-pervasive mood which heightened the energies of man and shaped a distinct style that differentiates the period so sharply from those which preceded and followed it.

It can be argued that at the point in time at which this volume begins the real thing was nearly over, and there was no more than an afterglow. In Germany, where Romanticism had become a religion, the ecstasies and transports had spent themselves well before 1815, driving not a few of their victims to an early death (Wackenroder and Novalis), to the madhouse (Hölderlin), or to suicide (Kleist). Those who survived – the Schlegels, Tieck, Adam Müller – were exhausted and had very little to say that was new. In England too, the Romantic poetry of the years after 1815 represented the last of several waves of this vast movement. The earliest Romantics (or 'pre-Romantics'), like Joseph Warton and Macpherson, were all dead; Wordsworth, Coleridge and Southey had their most creative phase behind them; and even the great meteors of around 1815 – Byron, Shelley and Keats – were dead by 1825. Only the minor figures, like the critics and essayists Hazlitt and De Quincey, remained. France was the only Western country in which there was a full-scale Romantic movement after 1815. The Polish, the Russian and, to some extent, the Italian Romantics, like the French, blossomed forth only in the second quarter of the century. But no one will deny that the impetus had come considerably earlier, first from England and then from Germany.

It may therefore seem legitimate to question the relevance of this chapter. But if, as stated earlier, this study is concerned with the trauma of the Revolution working itself out in a later generation, it is similarly motivated by an interest in the reverberations of the Romantic upheaval. This book has already put forward an interpretation of Romanticism as the sum total of the ways in which man's self-awareness was affected by the Revolutionary-Napoleonic disruption, and in which he tried to take his bearings in a world that had lost its 'fixities' and 'definities'. Man was at once a *révolté* and a creature craving some objective order; a being straining to express and assert itself and a soul yearning for self-surrender.

Romanticism, in the form of 'pre-Romanticism', started some fifty years before the Bastille was stormed. But the hands which razed the ancient fortress to the ground were directed by hearts and minds which had been formed gradually and for a long time before they rose in revolt. The Revolution had been well on the way before the waters rose to a flood in 1789. The same impulse – in different guises – was at work in the mounting spirit of Revolution as in the Romantic current.

Man wished to be free from restrictions imposed by religious tradition, political absolutism and a hierarchical social system in order to express and determine himself and create the kind of order in which he wished to live. That was the meaning of Romanticism on the social-political plane. In the personal context, man was visited by an urge to discover and recover his authentic self and to express it fully and creatively, instead of spinning the thread of tradition, subjecting himself to accepted conventions and fixed patterns, and imitating supposed models of perfection. That quest began in the middle of the eighteenth century. It was in itself a symptom of a loosening of 'fixities' and 'definities', and in turn came to act as a most effective solvent. When the undermined edifice came down with a crash, self-questioning turned into a frantic restlessness.

One of the most striking features of the early phase of the quest for authenticity was that it was started simultaneously by persons

87 The Romantic conception of the Bard, an ecstatic prophet alone in a wild natural landscape, high above the rest of humanity (see Ill. 63)

and groups in different parts of Europe, and often quite independently. Joseph Warton's *Enthusiast* appeared some ten years before Rousseau put pen to paper, and Rousseau was quite ignorant of the English pre-Romantic when he composed his two revolutionary *Discourses*. It would be an exaggeration to trace Herder's awakening on the Baltic coast and the *Sturm und Drang* ferment in Germany solely to the inspiration of English pre-Romanticism or the example of Rousseau; and German pietism was certainly a native growth. The antiquarian and Romantic preoccupation of Bodmer and Füssli in Switzerland were also at first a wholly local affair. Baal-Shem-Tov, the founder of Jewish Hassidism – the religion of the heart – in the remote vastnesses of south-east Galicia and Bukovina had never heard of Ossian's poetry or of the mystic Hamann. And yet they were all obeying the same impulse, the urge for free untrammelled self-expression, out of a protest against supposedly binding forms.

It was an uprising against rationalism, and yet in some ways the final consummation of a trend which had started with Luther and then issued into rationalism. In this respect the French enemies of Romanticism have a point when they place the responsibility for the madness at the doorstep of the German Reformation. At the same time Protestant and agnostic critics are of course right in stressing the affinities, and indeed the latter-day marriage, between Romanticism and Catholicism.

The Classical view is usually considered to be one which presupposes an objective, divine or rational order of 'unity, balance, harmony, completeness', into which we are born and against which the headstrong and rebellious may kick only at their peril and ultimately in vain. To the Romantic, on the other hand, the world and life are dissolved into an infinitude of stimuli, opportunities, challenges. If that is so, Luther's insistence on personal faith – as against the objective doctrines of the Church – was a first breach, and the Cartesian point of departure of radical doubt and individual discovery of truth followed from it. Yet neither Protestantism nor Rationalism ever doubted that, in spite of the individual method of searching after the truth, there *was* an objective truth, whether the Word of God or the tenets of reason.

88, 89  Two apostles of Romanticism. Rousseau (left) recorded his passions and despairs in his intimate *Confessions*. Goethe's *The Sorrows of Young Werther* became the bible of the young Romantics. The illustration above shows the suffering hero and a scene from his tragic love

This type of disciplined individualism was no longer enough for the Romantics. It came to mean to them no more than individually bowing to the same 'fixities' and 'definities'. And the Romantic craved not to find the same universal truth, but to experience reality in a way wholly his own. This was to be done not by reasoning, but through feeling, sentiment, imagination, instinct, passion, dream and recollection. These, unlike syllogistic reasoning, were modes of experience in each case spontaneous and unique: Goethe's *Werther* and Rousseau's *Nouvelle Héloïse* and *Confessions* are well-known examples. It has been suggested that the neo-Classical cult of Greek aesthetic perfection initiated by Winckelmann, to whom 'beauty [was] the perfect harmony of man with his destiny and of the parts to the whole', was also in fact a kind of liberation: a compensation for the cramped conditions of a sense-starved Protestant-sectarian existence: a shaft of light and beauty to redeem guilt-ridden men.

90 The Romantic Gothic revival. Pugin's visions of a Christian Gothic town were based on serious ethical-religious tenets and influenced the ideas of both Ruskin and Morris. He was responsible for part of the design of the Houses of Parliament

The quest for 'nature' and the 'natural' was pursued everywhere. It manifested itself as a preference for the rugged, wild and weird, as against the neatly artificial and tidy (the English as against the French garden); or for the simple, spontaneous and pristine – in brief, the genuine – as against the sophisticated, conventional, impure, and perhaps even the false and depraved. Such feelings were eloquent indications that reality had lost its obviousness and was no longer experienced naïvely and naturally as the air is breathed. This led to a revolution in taste. Symptomatic activities were: the search for, the

91, 92 Gustave Doré used his 'Gothick' imagination and grotesque fantasies mainly for book illustrations, such as this woodcut for Balzac's *Droll Stories*; in the background lies a medieval town (left). Right, a Gothic folly: the chapel in the garden of Strawberry Hill

rediscovery and, in the case of the Ossianic epics, the fabrication of ancient poetry; the publication of the Nibelungenlied and the Minne-singer; the interest in medieval vernacular romances and ballads about knights, ladies and love; and the new craze for Gothic architec-ture. In all this there was a desire to return beyond the tyrannically rigid rules of French classicism and to elevate spontaneous and native genius. Shakespeare was passionately admired: to Friedrich Schlegel 'das eigentliche Centrum, . . . Kern der romantischen Phantasie . . . gigantische Grösse der gothischen Heldenzeit'. The 141

93, 94   The Romantic glorification of the weird, demoniacal and mysterious led to a passion for ancient epics and the sprawling splendour of Shakespeare's genius. Below, Delacroix's etching of Hamlet confronted by his father's ghost; right, a typical Romantic vision of a ghostly moonscape, illustrating *Ossian*

vigour, the luxuriant and untidy abundance of Shakespeare, Cervantes, Calderon, Tasso and, of course, Dante, were placed above Homer and Virgil, the Classical models of allegedly ultimate, unsurpassable and solely valid perfection.

Not conscious and elaborate contrivance, but the free and irresistible flow of vital forces: here was a suggestion of mystery and miracle occurring again and again. While straining insatiably to experience every kind of sensation and all manner of feeling, the Romantic did not consider his soul a *tabula rasa* passively receiving random and disparate imprints from outside, but an immensely active energy, experiencing the infinitude of reality in a manner wholly his own and subjecting impressions to a metabolic process which turned them into an original creation. 'We receive but what we give. . . . A repetition in the finite mind of the eternal act of

creation in the infinite I AM', in the famous words of Coleridge. In brief, while the rationalist spoke of the rights of the individual, the Romantic glorified individuality. Where the former operated with the concept of man *per se*, the latter was obsessed with the unfathomable mystery and richness of the concrete personality.

All theory of art since Plato and Aristotle, with the possible exception of the comparatively brief period following the Renaissance, was based upon the idea that the essence of art was the imitation of external objects, with due regard to exigencies of theme, medium and response of the audience. 'An artist becomes possessed of the idea of that central form', says Reynolds, '. . . from which every deviation is deformity.' Johnson remarked that what is 'apart from adventitious and separable decorations and disguises . . . is common to human kind.' It was in the last decades of the eighteenth century

143

that writers began to apply the word 'expression', *Ausdruck*, to art, thinking solely of the artist's need for self-expression. To create was not to represent and describe but to press out something from within.

My friend, [says Werther] when darkness closes in upon my eyes, and the earth around me and heaven dwell in my soul like the form of a beloved mistress; then do I often think longingly: Oh couldst though only express, couldst thou breathe forth upon this paper, all that lives so full and warm in thyself, that it might become the mirror of thy soul, as thy soul is the mirror of the infinite God!

Developments in musical composition represented in the passage from Mozart to Beethoven had a powerful effect on nascent Romanticism.

When we listen to a sonata by Mozart, [writes Grout in his *History of Western Music*] we rejoice in the composer's constant and willing submission to an accepted order of things musical; when we listen to one of Beethoven's sonatas we rejoice that the revolutionist submits only where he pleases, and elsewhere he creates a new order, one growing out of the old but resembling it only in externals.

The young Wackenroder was smitten by the thought that if music – 'the movements of our spirit disembodied' – could not be reduced to mere imitation of outside sounds, but pointed to the self-sufficiency of the creative genius, the same must be true of all artistic creation.

This dualism of the artist, waiting to be visited, to be fructified by impressions and experiences, and of the demiurge who begets creations in his own inimitable and unalterable image, was symbolized by the Aeolian harp played upon by the wind.

Man [says Shelley] is an instrument over which a series of external and internal impressions are driven, like the alternations of an ever-changing wind over an Aeolian lyre, which move it by their motion to ever-changing melody. But there is a principle within the human being . . . which acts otherwise than in the lyre, and produces not melody alone, but harmony, by an internal adjustment of the sounds or motions thus excited to the impressions which excite them . . . give forth divinest melody, when the breath of universal being sweeps over their frame.

In this quest for spontaneity, immediacy and the plenitude of life Romanticism represents an extreme extension of the rationalist view of man as good, of the individual as supremely important, indeed sacred. But the conclusions drawn by Romanticism were quite anti-rationalist. The more direct, the less mediated man's urges and passions were, the more authentic and more valuable they appeared to the Romantics. Hence the apotheosis of the strange and bizarre, the eccentric and weird, the demoniacal and reckless. The centuries-old dualism of flesh and spirit, instinct and reason, nature and ethics was threatened by antinomianism. On the other hand, the straining for what was authentic and truly one's own led to an obsession with dreams, hallucination, somnambulism, hypnosis, and indeed with the bottomless abyss of the unconscious. It is enough to mention the early Coleridge and Blake, E. T. A. Hoffmann and Jean-Paul, and of course Novalis's *Hymns to the Night*. The human miracle of genius was absolved from all moral and other obligations, since the genius was a force of nature which 'bloweth where it listeth' ('der kein Gesetz über sich leidet').

95   E. T. A. Hoffmann saw the artist as possessed by demons. His nightmarish imagination and obsession with hallucinations mark all his stories. The legend beneath this illustration to his *Erzählungen* reads: 'A degenerate imagination's horrifying pictures of a seething mind – the terrifying children of madness'

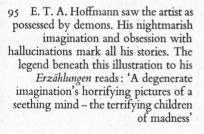

96, 97    Man versus infinity. C. D. Friedrich's *Man and Woman gazing at the Moon* shows two solitary humans in a supernatural, moonlit scene. Right, Turner's

In all this there lurked of course the danger of solipsism and utter individual isolation. An imminent breakdown of all forms threatened to destroy all possibilities of communication. This applied in particular to music and painting. Sculpture cannot be included because – significantly – Romanticism produced no sculpture, and only the spurious neo-Gothic in architecture. Eugénie de Keyser speaks in *The Romantic West* of 'music, which was so completely revolutionized by rich, complex orchestration, melodic eccentricities and the constant use of bizarre or incongruous harmonies'. The incomparable power of suggestion possessed by music, its ability to work on the mind directly without the mediation of words, and yet to convey an infinite range of impressions, feelings and thoughts,

tragic and magnificent vision of human helplessness before the fury of the elements, *Fire at Sea*

made it the ideal art of Romanticism. The dream of every poet and painter was to achieve the effect of music; he believed also that music somehow enables us to pierce the innermost mystery of the universe and to divest ourselves of all the chains holding us down.

As to painting, in the past the painter's aim had been not self-revelation but the discovery of an order which was warranted by the axiom of what de Keyser calls a 'rational link between the mind and the various phenomena it sought to analyse, isolate and comprehend', and was communicable with the help of a 'clear definition imparted to spatial structures by its perspective, which created a frame for the orderly disposition of well-defined subjects'. The cosmic vision of a Turner or a Corot disrupted these relationships:

'Objects lost their definition, the world its outlines.' All rational order dissolved in a subjective vision, in which nothing could be isolated to be analysed separately. As de Keyser writes:

Nothing was precisely located in space because everything was being used to create the effect of space. Outlines were fragmented by brush-strokes, and in the same way tricks of lighting were used to break up the composition or to connect objects that, seen objectively, would have been disparate. There was nothing pre-ordained about the world on the artist's canvas, for it was not objects themselves, now bereft of identity, that conveyed his message, but the way in which they were related.

The unresolved tension between the craving for an unlimited and infinitely varied experience and the apotheosis of individuality was also bound to produce a crisis of identity in the form of a paralysing neurosis of choice. Romanticism has been called by a hostile critic 'Occasionalismus', the lying in wait for occasions for experience. The world represents to the Romantic an infinitude of occasions for experience so that he may be able to test himself: 'The world must be romanticized,' says Novalis. 'Thus one recovers the original purport. . . . Romanticizing is nothing but the enhancement of potentiality.' The person obsessed by such a thought will never be able to make a choice: choosing from so many possibilities means in fact closing all avenues but one, without ever being sure whether the possibilities excluded might not have been vastly more exciting. Hence the suffused contours, the vague outlines, the autumnal mist, as against the clarity of outline and separation of objects in Classical art. Hence the Romantic predilection for the lyrical poem – the cry of the solitary – or for the fictional novel, preferably describing a wandering hero who undergoes the widest range of experience, and for the sonata or grand opera.

Thus the Romantic response could be twofold, either quietist – waiting for visitations to come – or unceasing, restless, striving. In both cases the original insistence on the concrete and immediate changed imperceptibly into a Platonic-mystical-Christian attitude: the disposition to treat the actual here and now as not truly real, but only as a murky reflection, a shadow, a symbol of something infinitely more meaningful and more sublime, to be indicated, suggested and communicated only in symbols. The actual, immediate and concrete turned as a result of this dialectic into external, finite signs of invisible, metaphysical connections. So much so that Novalis came to identify the Romantic and Christian attitudes as 'pure abstraction, withdrawal from the present, apotheosis of the future, that truly better world!', and similarly A. W. Schlegel, 'Contemplation of the infinite has destroyed the finite, life has become a world of shadow and night.'

The concomitant of this was that most distinctly Romantic feeling – infinite, never appeased longing, *Sehnsucht*. It might take the form of guilt and remorse-ridden, regretful nostalgia for some lost paradise of childlike innocence; of an often rebellious projection of passionate hope into the future; of yearning after distant lands, fairy-tale happenings, horrible deeds; or of an ivy-like clinging to ancient ruins, deserted castles, and graveyards.

To Friedrich Schlegel Classical art was that of 'contentment, untroubled by the smallest dis-ease, and in which not the slightest longing is experienced'. It was 'the poetry of possession' to his brother Wilhelm, whereas Romanticism was the poetry of longing. The former stood on the ground of the present, the latter swayed between recollection and atonement.

'Beethoven's music', writes E. T. A. Hoffmann, himself the myth- and legend-obsessed Romantic of Romantics, 'sets in motion the lever of fear, of awe, of horror, of suffering, and awakens just that infinite longing which is the essence of Romanticism. He is accordingly a completely Romantic composer.'

This striving after the unattainable explains Romantic irony and self-mockery: an attitude of both superiority and self-deprecation. The quest for identity brought home to the Romantics that self-identification meant establishing a relationship with others in love, friendship, marriage, society, and with the world in general: 'A frightful and yet fruitless yearning to spread out to the infinite and a burning eagerness to penetrate to the very heart of the individual.'

Friedrich Schlegel offers us again a deep insight into that tension between extreme egoistic introspection and the tremendous need to

149

become lovingly immersed into some vast One, whatever it might be, that would give certainty and security.

All my life and my years of philosophical discipleship have been filled with the ceaseless quest for the eternal unity of knowledge and love for a link to an external, historical reality or an ideal reality, at first the idea of a school and a new religion of ideas, then a link to the Orient, to Germany, to the liberty of poetry, finally to the Church, because without that the search for freedom and unity would be vain. Was that need for such a link not a need for protection, for a firm foundation?

This quest for self-identification was pursued under the impact of the convergence of vast forces, of which the most important was the French Revolution. With the exception of such odd-men-out as Edmund Burke, there was no enlightened person in Europe who did not greet the outbreak of the French Revolution as a glorious new dawn, or indeed as a final consummation. Then came the avalanche of kaleidoscopic and violent change, until all certainty was lost, not only as to what were the eternal and universal truths vouchsafed by the philosophers and made triumphant by the Revolution, but as to what man really was, and what he in fact wanted. Bewilderment and utter confusion followed in the ranks of the early admirers of the Revolution, including Wordsworth and Coleridge, as well as the German Romantics. Coleridge, for example, wrote:

Forgive me Freedom! O forgive me these dreams!
I hear thy voice, I hear thy loud lament

Add to this the bewildering impact of the Industrial Revolution, the severance of man from 'fixities' and 'definities', from the predictable run of rural existence, and the ensuing sense of alienation so poignantly expressed by William Blake in *Jerusalem*:

And all the Arts of Life they changed in to the Arts of Death.
The hour glass contemn'd because its simple workmanship
Was as the workmanship of the plowman, and the water
   wheel
That raises water into cisterns, broken and burn'd in fire

98 A page
from *Jerusalem*,
painted by
Blake himself

Because its workmanship was like the workmanship of the
 Shepherd;
And in their stead intricate wheels invented, wheel without
 wheel,
To perplex youth in their outgoings and to bind to labours in
 Albion
Of day and night the myriads of eternity, that they might file
And polish brass and iron hour after hour, laborious task,
Kept ignorant of its use: that they might spend the days of
 wisdom
In sorrowful drudgery to obtain a scanty pittance of bread,
In ignorance to view a small portion and think that All,
And call it Demonstration, blind to all the simple rules of life.

We need no more than mention here the escape from the cruelties of man into the bosom of never-changing, serene nature; of the comfort-giving Church, with its aesthetic splendours, sense of brotherhood and soothing charity; of the organic cohesion of the medieval hierarchical order; of the simplicities of folk-culture and the unswerving national tradition – 'the immortal life of the nation, generation linked to generation by faith, freedom, heraldry and ancestral fame . . .'; or even music: 'So I closed my eyes to all the strife and war in the world and retreated into the land of music as the land of faith, in which all our doubts and sorrows sink into a sea of sounds.' (E. T. A. Hoffmann)

Of greater interest to us are the more complex and more sophisticated responses. The personal inconsistencies and the vagaries of the Romantic, and the bewildering contradictions displayed by contemporary history, were sublimated into the famous theory of polarity, as dear to Coleridge as to the German Romantics: 'extremes meet'. Out of the tension between the opposites there would emerge something which was both a synthesis and something quite new. This was a process which could never come to an end. Conception occurred as a result of clash and fusion, and birth through break and pain. The most real thing in the universe was thus the fact of becoming and not of being, of activity and not completion, of endless longing and not of 'quietude and collectedness of mind'. The mechanical and atomistic philosophy which envisaged particles propelled by motion and coming into contact or collision was replaced by the idea of process – as partly suggested by the contemporary developments in biology, geology and psychology. The emphasis upon mathematical relationships and the image of separate parts fitting into a static pattern gave way to the vision of organic growth and development from the embryo to the fully unfolded personality, and the laws of nature came to be manifested in the interaction between accidents from outside and the peculiar nature of the object.

The Cartesian-Newtonian pattern had been closely connected with the associationist psychology of Locke, Hartley and Condillac. To Coleridge this 'necessitarianism' was a theory of darkness and death, since it spelled human bondage. It viewed men as passive recipients of sensations, all of whose thoughts were in fact no more than recollections or rearrangements of external impressions. For the Romantics such a theory broke up life into fragments and subjected man to a hopeless determinism. Kant and science combined to shape an anti-associationist philosophy which interpreted man much as the Romantics interpreted the artist – as one who created rather than merely producing variations of what was known.

Kant made man the legislator of nature, the judge who knows how to extract answers from nature by asking the right questions, and Fichte turned all external being into spiritual self-awareness, all knowledge into self-knowledge, and the external world into the achievement of human liberty. Fichte's *Wissenschaftslehre* was singled out by Schlegel as one of the three parents of Romanticism, alongside the French Revolution and Goethe's *Wilhelm Meister*. The momentous developments in science which occurred at that very time were indeed increasingly based not on mere observation of external phenomena with the help of the senses, but on the use of instruments to record things beyond the perception of the senses. Examples are the discovery of ultra-red and ultra-violet by Herschel and Ritter, and the advances made in the investigation of electricity, magnetism and the structure of the atom. A little later scientists would begin to create 'pure' laboratory situations which did not exist in nature at all, and would deal with relationships between phenomena in the abstract language of mathematical formulae. Philosophical knowledge, ethical perfection, and scientific truth were as a result beginning to be seen not as something to be acquired once and for all, but as objects of Romantic striving which could have no end, an aspiration approaching its never-attainable goal only through the substitution, or indeed negation, of one achieved stage by a higher one.

Kant felt the necessity, but was unable, to prove the reality of purpose and organic totality, just as in his theory of ethics he failed to go beyond a certain atomism. Although he rejected the utilitarianism and hedonism of self-interest, he never succeeded – as Schiller felt so strongly – in binding men with the tie of love, in addition to

99　The desolation of Stonehenge with its majestic stones open to the elements suited the mood of Constable in his troubled later years

the sense of imperative duty towards each other. The organic community and purposeful organic unity both remained postulates.

It was a most important fact, however, that Kant lifted both the ethical postulate and the concept of organic purpose out of the domain of natural, predetermined necessity and the scientific chain of causation. Since there were no ethics without moral responsibility, the freedom of the human will, which could not be proven scientifically, was an absolute necessity. Therefore, there was a kingdom of free human ends, and a world that had a meaning and a purpose, and was not a mere mechanism. This became the great inspiration to the Romantic poets and seers: to convey to men living in darkness and listless distraction that sense of togetherness and interconnectedness, which they themselves were able to experience so vividly at the moment of creative ecstasy and outgoing love.

In lines which have today a highly topical ring, Shelley formulates the challenge held out to the poet by a world in which rapid change and growing multiplicity, contradiction and conflict, have not only destroyed the sense of ontological unity but also all moral certainty and social sentiment. 'The cultivation of poetry is never more to be desired', he writes, 'than at periods when, from an excess of the selfish and calculating principle, the accumulation of the materials of external life exceeds the quantity of the power of assimilating them to the internal laws of human nature. The body has then become too unwieldy for that which animates it.'

Symphonic music, just at that time celebrating its greatest triumphs, was again called in as evidence that the whole comes before the parts, and was not just assembled from separate pieces. What music stood for in the southern Catholic countries was expressed by painting, above all landscape painting, in the north – Turner and Constable in England, Friedrich and Runge in Germany.

100 *Rest on the Flight into Egypt*. Runge tried in his paintings to recapture the innocence of childhood and communion with nature

It is enough to allude to the place of nature and landscape in nine-teenth-century music from Beethoven's *Pastoral Symphony* onwards.

It was the heightened energy of the soul, that Romantic overflow of feeling, rather than discursive reasoning that enabled some of the Romantics to make the leap into religious faith. It enabled others to obtain a vivid, all-pervading sense of communion with Nature as one great organism, with Universal Life at its source: 'a sense of the Whole as a living unity, a sense of God in all and all in God'. This 'All' is not 'an immense heap of *little* things', but 'that something great, something one and indivisible', which Coleridge's 'mind feels as if it ached to behold and know': Coleridge's 'reason and imagination' as distinguished from mere syllogistic understanding.

The imagination of the age had been captured by the astounding developments in electro-magnetism, from Volta, Galvani and Ritter via Ampère, Örsted and Faraday to the discovery by Mayer and Helmholtz in the 1840s of the epoch-making second law of thermo-dynamics on the conservation of energy. Observation of the effects of electric current upon human muscles and nerves, and then the discovery of the possibility of storing up and employing electric energy as power that impels and produces chemical changes in the affected objects, engendered the idea of a universal life-force at work in all phenomena – mechanical, physical and chemical – in organic as well as inorganic nature. An example is Schelling's *Naturphilosophie*, concerning the *Weltseele* or the *All-Leben*, and his belief that nature is 'objective reason', 'a frozen intelligence . . . with all its sensations and views . . . manifestation of the spirit', and human consciousness an outgrowth of nature become history. It placed in a new light the question of body and soul, directly in-fluencing medicine and psychology, for instance, by pointing to the interdependence of the physiological, mental and psychological elements. The faculty of reason no longer stood out alone, in a permanent struggle to become disengaged from influences – of the senses, emotions and fancies – which obscure and hamper clear per-ception. Abstract logic was to give way to concrete logic of the con-crete concatenation. 'Thinking', says Novalis, 'is only a dream of feeling, an extinct feeling, only grey, weakly living.'

Are we still, in the light of the Romantic dilemma of the One and
the Many, entitled to distinguish between a revolutionary or progressive and a reactionary or quietist strand in Romanticism? In a
sense every variety of Romanticism was a protest, even the various
conservative versions. For surely the reactionary tendencies of German
Romanticism in the later years of the French Revolution and under
Napoleon were an expression of resistance to a conquering and
dominant force as well as support for the established order. The
revival of religion, and especially of sympathy for Catholicism and
its cultural and artistic heritage, was in no small measure due to the
sorry fate of monasteries and their artistic treasures – first under the
Revolution in France and then in Germany when the ecclesiastical
states were mediatized. This is noticeable in both German Romanticism and in Chateaubriand's *Génie du Christianisme*, which is a
hymn to the beauties and consolations of Christianity rather than
a theological apologia. The same may be said of the evolution of
Wordsworth, Coleridge and Southey from Jacobins into Tories.
After the fall of Napoleon, radical anti-Tory revolutionary Romanticism made its mighty voice heard in Byron and Shelley. The same
was true in France: Mme de Staël and Chateaubriand fought
Napoleon, but the great Romantics of the next generation, like
Lamartine and Victor Hugo, started as legitimists but ended up
under the July Monarchy as Republicans and social radicals. What
could be a more striking evolution than the metamorphosis of
Lamennais from the most fanatical ultramontane into the apostle of
the Red revolution?

And yet the fact remains that with the uncharacteristic exception of Heine, the age of reaction in Germany threw up no
major *révolté* of Romantic provenance. National character and
tradition count for something in this. The two prototypes of
the Promethean myth in modern times came from the German
world: Beethoven and Fichte (even if we exclude Faust, again a
German). Their example, however, was emulated not in Germany,
but by Byron, Mazzini, Mickiewicz, and in a minor key by the
French poets.

Napoleon described his feelings on the Arcoli bridge as a sense of being lifted up into space, and when asked whether he would like to be God himself, replied, 'No, that is a cul-de-sac.' Another Romantic dimension was then added to the image: the captive hero chained to a rock in a lonely island in the far Atlantic – the modern Prometheus, the saviour of mankind, liberator of nations. In the stirring first chapter of the *Confessions d'un enfant du siècle* Alfred de Musset gives an unforgettable evocation of the pale-faced youth abandoning himself avidly to the 'mal du siècle' out of despair at the lost glories of the Napoleonic saga. After these are passed in review, there follows the tiresome clinical analysis of a man and woman interlocked in an impossible relationship à la *Adolphe* of Benjamin Constant. Both these motives are wonderfully represented in French literature of the first half of the century. Stendhal's Julien Sorel is the plebeian conqueror who embodies that aspiration for equality which, in fact, hides the irresistible urge to show oneself inferior to none in variety and intensity of experience, and so indeed superior to the whole world. Karl Marx justly admired Balzac's heroes as bourgeois Napoleons driven on by the demon of Mammon, the acquisitive spirit becoming a kind of idealism, a whip, a passion and a snare – in brief, poetry. The salvationist theme finds a less differentiated, a rather gently loving and sweetly hopeful tone in Lamartine's odes prophesying universal reconciliation, like the significantly entitled *Marseillaise de la Paix*. The apogee is reached in Victor Hugo's self-sacrificing, superhuman heroes, hastening to succour the oppressed and the humiliated against overdrawn strange settings which call for the brush of a Delacroix and the over-abundant orchestration of Berlioz; and in the generous and impulsive George Sand who narrowly escaped prison in 1848 for incitement to rebellion against a lawful parliamentary majority.

How the same frame of mind may result in different and even contrasted attitudes is shown in juxtaposing Novalis, and still more Schleiermacher, with Shelley and Byron. There is no more eloquent analysis of the religious sentiment as a sense of absolute dependence on the Cosmic One and nowhere could we find a more poetic suggestion of communion with the All, both the visible and

101   Napoleon's career fired the imagination of the young Romantics, and painters such
as Baron Gros contributed even more than poets to the myth which grew about him

102, 103, 104 Three Romantic poets. Novalis, the mystic visionary; Heine, the ironic lyric poet; and the expatriate Polish patriot Adam Mickiewicz

invisible, than in Novalis. And Schleiermacher writes:

I am lying in the bosom of the infinite universe, I am at this moment its soul, because I feel all its force and its infinite life as my own. It is at this moment my own body, because I penetrate all its limbs as if they were my own, and its innermost nerves move like my own [*nach meinem Sinn und Ahndung*]. . . . Try out of love for the universe to give up your own life. Strive already here to destroy your own individuality and to live in the One and in the All . . . fused with the Universe.

Almost all German Romantics ended as upholders of medievalism, at most tempering the indolence of pantheistic self-abandon with reminders of the need for Christian self-improvement through Christian self-discipline. By contrast, the pantheist Shelley becomes the Godwinian author of *Prometheus Unbound*, the *Revolt of Islam* and *The Mask of Anarchy* – hymns of Messianic, revolutionary universalism; while Byron becomes the prophet and law-giver of revolutionary Romanticism on the Continent. The imagination of European youth, in the first place of the eternally young Goethe, was caught by the prototype of the *poète maudit*, devoured by furies from within, the hell inside, the outcast restlessly on the move, the

rebel and enemy of all complacency, establishment and self-satis-
faction, hastening to an early death for the sake of Greek liberty.
Byron writes in *Childe Harold's Pilgrimage*:

> For what is Poesy but to create
> From overfeeling, Good and Ill, and aim
> At an external life beyond our fate,
> And be the new Prometheus of new man,
> Bestowing fire from heaven, and then, too late,
> Finding the pleasure given repaid with pain.

Donning the mantle of Byron, the Polish poet Mickiewicz shakes
off the personal preoccupations of an unhappy lover and assumes
all the guilt and all the sorrows of his martyred nation, taking on the
awful responsibility of prophet-leader. He dies in 1854 in Constantinople, trying to raise a Polish Legion to fight against the Tsar
alongside the Crimean powers. .

105 Beethoven
embodied the
Promethean myth
of the artist
in conflict
with society

The later fortunes of German Romanticism therefore appear all the more baffling and more paradoxical as compared with the Western varieties. With all its rebelliousness and revolutionary activism, Western Romanticism remained true to the Classical tradition of our civilization, whereas the yielding, self-effacing pantheistic quietism of the Germans became a demoniacally destructive force.

Heinrich Heine was vouchsafed an uncanny prophetic insight into the terrifying potentialities of German Romantic pantheism, with its vision of man as a being swallowed up or impelled by cosmic forces, the all-embracing Will of History, and the destiny of the Race. These were the favourite images of the various architects of catastrophe, who never tired of pouring scorn on the bloodless, cogitating, analysing and vacillating creature cut off from the vital forces of being. Heine himself was a Goya-like sample of Romanticism, the crucified Jew lying paralysed and in agony on his mattress. He was the very embodiment of Romantic irony: mercilessly scoffing at all the national sanctities of German Romanticism, he was in fact hopelessly in love with them. But to him, an outcast Jew, these were still more unattainable than to the fair-haired and blue-eyed Teutons. The more poignant his longing, the more self-lacerating his irony. A man hungry for recognition and admiration, he had a worthless ignorant wife whom he loved to distraction and who was unable to understand a word of his poetry. And what a manifestation of the superiority of the human spirit over all the powers of the cosmos was the poetic triumph of the dying man!

'A LIGHT, A GLORY...'

Modern man and contemporary civilization are inconceivable without the Romantic ingredient. The Classical type – according to Goethe, himself an unwilling Romantic – was content to reach the ante-chamber of the holy truth; modern man, on the other hand, has an obsessive urge for authentic self-expression and a Faustian need to penetrate into the heart of the innermost mystery of the All and the Whole. Equally Romantic in origin are the eternal rebelliousness of the self-alienated and dissatisfied, and the loving self-identification of the Prometheans with the collective soul of the universe, nature, history, the nation, the church, the class, the revolution. Schopenhauer, Nietzsche, Kierkegaard, Van Gogh were of the first type; Cardinal Newman, Carlyle, Bakunin and Jaurès of the second.

The Romantic dichotomy of the unique and the universal, the concrete and the ideal, was sublimated in the idolization of history. The pious interest in concrete detail, the affectionate search for the pristine and unique have given us those limpid studies of the foundations of European civilization and of the various national histories, their earliest social structure, institutions, laws and ideas. The Romantic rejection of the dualism of soul and body, reason and the life of the senses and instincts, made real history possible. Events were no longer submitted to and judged according to universal and abstract criteria, but considered on their own merits, and by the light of their own concrete logic, in which reason and instinct, idealism and selfishness, the rational and the contingent, past and present are indissolubly fused. This bestowed upon the writings of Michelet, Ranke and Augustin Thierry a wonderful freshness, but also very often indeed a dangerously misleading seductiveness. Nations, ages, classes were endowed with a soul, were depicted as driven by a destiny, as unconsciously realizing vast goals across the ages. The French Revolution became to Michelet the Second Coming of Christ: the Bastille falls because of its tormented conscience, the people emerge as the real hero of history. Ranke saw the great powers interlocked in permanent struggle, each representing a living principle of its own. In Thierry's view all history had been waiting for the arrival of the communes and the reassertion of the Celtic substratum against the Teutonic upper crust. More than that, the need to reconcile the concrete and the universal, the Many and the One, historical continuity and revolutionary break, produced those grandiose visions of historical inevitability, in which the particular found its necessary place in the vast scheme of Time, embracing all the concatenations of fleeting circumstances in an iron logic. Hegel and Marx were unthinkable in the earlier centuries. History either had a linchpin in providence or ran in cycles. And who will deny that all the modern

163

ideologies – all of which, incidentally, emerged in the age of Romanticism – are in essence visions of history?

It was youthful exuberance that made men see things as twice their size, employ flamboyant language and imagery, work themselves up into fiery passion and ascribe vastly exaggerated significance to their own generous impulses and dreams, as well as to the obtuseness, inertia, recalcitrance or ordinary meanness of the forces opposed to them.

Of course, there was inflated rhetoric and theatrical pose, makebelieve and often an inability to act verging on characterlessness. Yet all these were the distortions of something fundamentally noble. No one seems to have grasped and depicted this better than Gustave Flaubert, the supposed realist, in his great novel on the Romantic age and 1848, *L'Education sentimentale*. Seemingly a scathing satire, it is in truth an elegy. The romantic, beautiful and pure heroine is a mere shadow. She and her lover are pining away their years, while she has to share her bed with a sordid and contemptible bourgeois husband, and he is morbidly driven to consort with a shabby whore whom he despises. Frédéric is chasing after phantoms – the ideal woman and the idea worth dying for. But when Paris is aflame with revolution, he eats out his soul in the arms of his unloved mistress miles away, hearing the faint sounds of firing on the Paris boulevards. On the other hand, the eloquent talkers of revolution are overcome by a strange paralysis during the terrible days of June, and are afterwards unable to bear the withering dumb look of the proletarian captives from their cages. A story of utter futility? No doubt. Yet the heroine is beautiful and compelling in spite of being virtually featureless, and neither she nor her lover fail to wring our hearts. The mood of *L'Education sentimentale* is not one of contempt and condemnation, but of infinite regret: it might have been, it could have been, but it was not.

With Romanticism there died something which men have never been able to recapture. Coleridge describes it as:

A light, a glory, a fair luminous cloud enveloping the earth . . . that from the soul itself must issue forth . . . , the original gift of spreading the tone, the atmosphere, and with it the depth and height of the ideal world around forms, incidents and situations, in which for the common view, custom had bedimmed all the lustre, had dried up the sparkle and the dewdrops. It is not merely that in middle and old age one is no longer able to experience the sense of wonderment and thrill at novelty which is the gift of the young, of the poet and the seer:

the charm of novelty to things of every day . . . a feeling analogous to the supernatural, by awakening the mind's attention from the lethargy of custom and directing it to the loveliness and the wonders of the world before us; an inexhaustible treasure, but for which, in consequence of the film of familiarity and selfish solicitude we have eyes, and see not, ears that hear not, and hearts that neither feel nor understand.

We have come to feel with the ageing Coleridge:

I see them all, so exactly fair,
I see, *not feel*, how beautiful they are.

That capacity for joy, 'joy the luminous cloud', is gone.

Well might the Romantic groan with Byron 'I am born a child of wrath', 'be thy proper hell', and with Blake, 'a hell of terrors and horrors . . . in a divided existence'. Well might he wallow in remorse, ennui and self-pity. All the same he was filled with a profound sense of the sublime seriousness of life. The angry prophet in him might fulminate, threaten and castigate, strike attitudes and poses; he would still overflow – in the words of Wordsworth – with 'the joy of that pure principle of love . . . a holy tenderness pervade his frame!'

In the midst of an immense wasteland, joy has changed for us into anxiety, and exaltation into devouring self-contempt, and faith has given way to a paralysing sense of ambivalence that breeds cynicism and despair.

Though I should gaze for ever
On that green light that lingers in the west:
I may not hope from outward forces to win
The passion and the life, whose fountains are within.

A SPECTRE BECOMES FLESH

When speaking of the spectre haunting Europe, the authors of the *Communist Manifesto* in 1847 had no idea that within a few months the spectre would become flesh and the Revolution sweep across Europe with lightning speed, encountering hardly any resistance, cowing kings and putting omnipotent statesmen to flight. The prophets of the Revolution one and indivisible seemed to be proved right beyond all expectations, and no Romantic imagination could have envisaged such a spectacular, dramatic and convincing manifestation of the workings of an all-embracing dialectic in history, with a definite rhythm of its own. And therefore all the more striking, the more bewildering were the speed and ease with which, within a few months, these revolutions were everywhere overcome. How are we to explain this easy triumph and speedy disaster, and to evaluate the legacy of that year which started with such fair and generous hopes and ended in frustration, despair and exacerbated hatreds?

Many factors caused general unrest in 1847-8: the disastrous harvest of 1847; the potato famine; the grave economic crisis which gripped Europe; the series of banquets in support of franchise reform in France; the troubles which broke out in January in Sicily, followed by isolated disturbances (the 'tobacco revolt') in northern Italy. But none of these in themselves account for the practically simultaneous outbreak and rapid spread of the Revolution. The trauma of revolution was the underlying cause. The universal expectation of revolution gave wings to the hopeful as soon as the signs began to appear propitious. It overwhelmed the fearful with panic, followed by a fatalistic resignation as soon as their grip began to falter. This is how small-scale *émeutes* swelled into revolution, and why Metternich, Louis-Philippe and Guizot gave up so quickly,

166

106  Daumier's symbol of the Republic as a majestic divinity, both chaste and fertile  ▶

enjoining those whom they abandoned to bow with good grace to the inevitable; and the same is true of all the other kings, kinglets, princes and potentates.

A spontaneous mass uprising, or the contrivance of some demagogues and underground plotters? In the seemingly quiet 'forties (as distinct from the 'hungry 'forties' in England) a fairly large proportion of the population had become saturated with liberal, democratic and indeed socialist ideas. True, the wave of civil disturbance and riot had subsided in France after the pathetic failure of the operatic *coup* of Blanqui and Barbès on a sunny Sunday afternoon in 1839, in the sight of promenading Parisians. But if repression decimated the ranks of revolutionary activists, it also brought about a kind of natural selection: the most determined went underground and evolved into a hardened fighting vanguard.

In Paris, as well as in other capitals, there were in February 1848 multitudes whose respect for the powers that be and faith in the justice and durability of the social order had been greatly undermined. At the same time their sympathies had been stirred in favour of the victims of political persecution. Small groups of men – members of secret societies, artisans, workers and students – knew very well what they wanted. Their *élan* was to grow into a ferocious resolve, once they felt sympathetic crowds behind them, pressing forward in front of the Palais-Bourbon, the Royal Palace in Berlin, the University in Vienna.

The romanticized imagination of the period curiously distorted the realities of the situation in the minds of men on the eve of, and, still more, during the February Revolution. It resulted in eloquent make-believe, massive insincerities and much shadow-boxing.

Tocqueville had warned the Orléans régime that a Chamber elected on a narrow franchise, with deputies belonging to the same class, engaging in debates and controversies which were not the expression of fundamentally different interests but a kind of airy art-for-art's-sake politics, would make the parliamentary system appear at best a show unconnected with genuine issues, at worst an assembly of large shareholders. It would thus widen the dangerous gap between the *pays légal* and the *pays réel*. It is curious to observe how, in a resolve to appear as a government of national reconciliation, a system of *juste milieu* and bourgeois sobriety helped to feed the mood of romantic exaltation by bringing over the remains of Napoleon for national burial and by giving free rein to the cult of the Revolutionary myth. Lamartine's *History of the Girondins* and the first volume of Michelet's *History of the French Revolution* were tremendously effective tableaux of the Revolution. Neither the authors nor their avid readers really desired a repetition of those bloody events. But the drama, the colour, the gnashing of teeth, the glorious eloquence, the beautiful deaths and the clash of mighty, super-personal forces depicted on broad canvas emphasized the pusillanimity and pedestrian character of the régime of the day. Such a régime appeared to be almost a national dishonour.

Jacobin patriotism was in the fortunate position of being able to identify the national glory of France with a universal mission as the liberator of oppressed nations. It was not only the myth of 1792–3. There was also the community of interests between France, which was humiliated in 1815, and all those unhappy nations which were groaning under the yoke of the enemies of France. So the reassertion of France's greatness was bound up with a European revolution led by Paris.

This was precisely the spectre that haunted Louis-Philippe, who was more than anything anxious to be recognized as an equal among the royal cousins of Europe. In the 1830s there had been an uneasy *entente* between the two constitutional monarchies – France and Britain – in support of Belgium and the unhappy Iberian queens against their reactionary usurping uncles supported by the Holy Alliance. But Guizot, Louis-Philippe's Prime Minister, became more and more resolved to strengthen the forces of order against the revolutionary hydra, to the point of aligning himself with the Holy Alliance powers against the democratic cantons of Switzerland in their struggle with the centrifugal aspirations of the Catholic Sonderbund. Where she did not actively collaborate with the reactionary monarchies, France gave way to them on almost every issue or, as in the case of the Eastern Question, to the European powers combined.

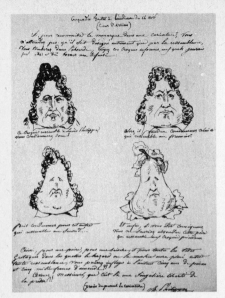

107, 108  A caricature demonstrating Louis-Philippe's resemblance to a pear – which in vernacular French means a dolt (left). The minister Guizot (right) incarnated the resistance of the French government to liberal reform of the constitution

Frigidly upright and contemptuously unruffled, Guizot dismissed the demand for a wider franchise as an artificial agitation started by busy-bodies. As late as 22 February Louis-Philippe was still nonchantly shrugging his shoulders at 'urchins' excitement'. Within hours the principle of popular sovereignty based on universal and equal suffrage was for the first time in history accepted by absolutely everybody as a sacrosanct and self-evident truth. A wave of brotherly solidarity swept France. Priests were blessing trees of liberty. In an excess of egalitarian solidarity the rich were seeking out poor relatives and donning proletarian caps. All were pledging themselves to put an end to social injustice forthwith.

FROM GENERAL CONCORD TO CLASS WAR – FRANCE

Yet from the very start there was the unsolved question of a political-democratic revolution faced with pressure for a social revolution. Or to put it differently: democratic parliamentary legitimacy was confronted by the insistence on the absolute validity of a revolutionary final goal, without reference to the counting of heads.

170

The Republic was proclaimed from the balcony of the Hôtel de Ville, where the democratic deputies had assembled in the revolutionary tradition at the behest of Lamartine, the eloquent Romantic poet who was for a time the outstanding figure of the Revolution. It was he who had dashed the hopes for a regency on behalf of Louis-Philippe's grandson, pathetically brought into the Chamber by his beautiful widowed mother. The demand to proclaim the Republic was at first resisted on the grounds that that was a matter for the whole people to decide, and that it would be an act of usurpation to present the sovereign people with a *fait accompli*. But the ardent revolutionaries had their way, after reproaching the official leaders with lack of conviction: they had dared to depose Louis-Philippe without an explicit mandate, yet now displayed a mortifying lack of self-assurance, as if the Republic was not something obvious and sacrosanct, but needed a special vote to become so.

Swearing again by the sacred principle of universal suffrage, Lamartine at first opposed proclamation of the right to work:

109   Lamartine addresses the people of Paris on 25 February 1848

apart from any question of its validity, it was outside the competence of the provisional government. He and his colleagues ended by hurriedly conceding the point, as well as agreeing a few days later to the establishment of national workshops to absorb the unemployed, and to a parliament of Labour to sit at the Palais du Luxembourg under the presidency of the reluctantly co-opted socialist minister, Louis Blanc. These shifts could easily be made to appear as deep plotting. The socialists were naturally inclined to interpret half-hearted pledges and makeshift stratagems – designed to escape violence and gain time – as measures of world renovation and first instalments in a total social transformation. This made the political democrats impatient with their socialist allies and guiltily angry with themselves. The bourgeois parties became anxious to hasten the convocation of a Constituent Assembly; a state of emergency invited pressure and violence, and must be replaced by a system of universally recognized legitimacy. The apostles of social revolution – Blanqui and others – insisted on postponing the elections, if possible *sine die*. They claimed that majorities wrested from an immature people, still suffering the trauma of bondage and not yet fully conscious of its rights and powers, were a fraud. Such majorities could not be invoked against the objective, deep-seated will of the people and the decrees of history embodied in the revolutionary vanguard – the executor of the Will of Time armed with unlimited rights and powers.

The elections gave a clear majority to the moderate republicans. The radical Jacobins and socialists could see no hope of making their revolution triumph except through a revolutionary dictatorship. A terrorist dictatorship was, however, impossible without the atmosphere created by a terrible national emergency, such as war. This was as well understood by Lamartine, the virtual head of the Provisional Government and its Foreign Minister, as by Blanqui, the prophet of the violent revolution and dictatorship. From the start, Lamartine was determined to prevent the Republic from embarking upon a revolutionary crusade, as his studiously ambiguous manifesto to the powers of Europe amply shows. Blanqui pressed for war on behalf of the oppressed peoples – in the first place, the

Poles. A revolutionary war was calculated to bring the most radical revolutionaries to the fore, in France as well as in all other countries seething with revolution, while national isolationism was sure to cause the revolutionary unrest to work itself out within narrow confines. The European revolution could not, in the best of circumstances, come to fruition without a victorious war against Russia, the only guardian of monarchist legitimacy which had remained unaffected by the general European conflagration. Fittingly, a mass demonstration (15 May) on behalf of the Poles and calling for an immediate declaration of war on the Tsar, came to end with the proclamation of a revolutionary government in place of the parliamentary government, and the 'dissolution' of the frightened Chamber. Within a few hours of the demonstration the ringleaders were rounded up, and an irresistible wave of reaction set in.

As a result of the revolution, the economic life of France had come to a standstill and the population had ceased to pay taxes. The numbers of the inmates of the national workshops maintained at government expense mounted and mounted, until they reached the frightening figure of over 110,000. When the government had grudgingly and rather unthinkingly given their approval to the idea – 'sold' to them by an unknown young engineer of twenty-five, called Thomas – they had envisaged a figure of some 10,000 only. They had borne in mind the possibility of using these workers as a praetorian guard in an emergency. Now the workers seemed more like a potential army of the Red revolution, demoralized by idleness and political agitation, and paid for out of an empty Treasury at the expense of the propertied classes whom their serried ranks might overwhelm any day. The bourgeoisie was filled with dumb fear and grew resolved to 'put an end to it' and dissolve the nest of anarchy and rebellion immediately. The workers, sensing the designs of government, and feeling cheated and betrayed, began to harbour desperate thoughts.

And so it came to the terrible blood-bath of June 1848, the 'slave war'. The workers' rising was ruthlessly crushed; the Red menace was overcome in the very city where, only four months before, it had reared its victorious head. The new barbarians, as Tocqueville

# LE SALUT PUBLIC.

remarked, had spread a fear and terror among the propertied and the civilized unknown since the invasion of Rome by the hordes from the north. Now, frightened out of its wits and weighed down by a guilty conscience, the French bourgeoisie abandoned itself to an orgy of Red-baiting. The 'right to work' was rejected. Treated by the speakers of the Right to the vilest insults, the workers were conceded no more than a right to Christian charity. The June Days in Paris had immense repercussions all over Europe. In February, Paris gave the sign to begin the Revolution; in June it provided an example of the way to liquidate it.

### CONFLICT OF NATIONS: MITTELEUROPA

If the fortunes of the February Revolution in France revealed the abyss between image and reality in the social sphere of class war, the vicissitudes of the March Revolution in Germany and Austria were a lesson in the intractable nature of nationalist conflict.

, III The tri-
ph of the people,
nce 1848. Left,
urbet's heroic
rkmen on the
ricades; the ban-
reads 'voice of
d, voice of the
ople'. Right,
umier's vision of
is street urchins
the throne-room
the Tuileries
ace

The close connection between the constitutional issue and national aspirations was demonstrated in the earliest stage of the Revolution all over Germany. Frederick William IV in almost the same breath promised a constitution and proclaimed that Prussia would thenceforth relinquish her separate existence and share the fate of Germany as a whole. This was not necessarily a ruse on the part of the impressionable and neurotic king, whose head, his courtiers complained, was constructed differently from the heads of other people. When he uncovered it in front of the funeral cortège of the revolutionaries who fell storming his palace, he was in all probability at that moment feeling deeply moved.

The victory of constitutionalism in all the German states was immediately followed by a meeting of representatives of legislative assemblies, the initiative for which had already been taken by the southern political leaders before the outbreak of the Revolution. They deliberated about ways of uniting Germany from below rather

175

than from above; or rather through agreement between princes and subjects, the princes among themselves, and the peoples among themselves. Like France in the early days of the February Revolution, Germany was swept by an illusion of universal concord, which in this case proved to be the undoing of the Revolution.

The all-too-easy surrender of the entrenched powers and their seemingly sincere reconciliation with the new state of things appeared to make a thorough sweep and a revolutionary overhaul unnecessary. Kings could be left on their thrones; the old armies, the officer corps, the police, the civil service could be left intact and at the disposal of the princes – surrounded now, after all, by ministers, like Camphausen, who enjoyed popular backing and could be trusted to act as faithful guardians of the new constitutions. The German liberals would have balked at the idea of forceful and summary action. Kantian insistence on mutual respect for reciprocal rights and faith in the power of rational argument combined with a deep horror of violence and disorder, which was regarded as not merely morally wrong, but positively squalid.

112  After initial phrase-making about his 'beloved Berliners' on the outbreak of the March Revolution, Frederick William IV ordered the Prussian military to crush the remnant of the scattered revolutionary movement

113, 114 A demagogue (below) and a barricade in a working-class district of Berlin during the riots of 18–19 March 1848

Only the extreme Left and, as was soon shown, the extreme Right, were free from such illusions; only they fully grasped the ultimate significance of power. The Left were obsessed by the conviction that no class ever willingly gave up its power. The Right, above all Bismarck, were motivated by utter contempt for the common run of men: selfish, muddle-headed, vain, weak-minded and infirm of will, they had to be forcefully confronted with *faits accomplis*. Once the Junkers recovered from the initial shock and realized that the revolutionary hydra was not invincible, they resolved, in the words of their master, Frederick William IV, that 'only soldiers help against the democrats'. The realization of the ultimate significance of power was behind the agitation unchained by the extreme Left in favour of war. The radicals in Germany had still stronger reasons than the French extremists for wanting war. A war against Russia and for the liberation of Poland was calculated to become a people's war under a terrorist dictatorship in a German Republic, one and indivisible. For a moment even a man like von Arnim, the new Prussian Foreign Minister, toyed with the idea of

177

war in the east. What Bismarck accomplished twenty-two years later in the west, Arnim and his followers hoped to achieve on the plains of Poland: the rallying of all German states under Prussia in a national war. Neither Lamartine, nor of course the Prussian King, brother-in-law of Nicholas I, whose father had saved Prussia from extinction in 1807, could ever consent to such a venture in the midst of not merely a political, but also a social revolution.

Also from the point of view of the aspirations to national unity, therefore, the most important fact in the situation after March 1848 was that all the German states remained separate and intact, and that in each of them the apparatus of power remained in the same hands. For those in power were the people whose very existence was threatened by the unification of Germany.

While the dynastic principle continued to be, in spite of new constitutions, the basis of particularism, representatives of the German nation as a whole assembled in Frankfurt, first as a Vorparlament consisting of representatives of the diets, then as the all-German Assembly elected directly by the nation to deliberate on the problem of unification. The two assemblies comprised some of the finest minds and loftiest spirits of Germany, and felt fortified by the right – as representatives of the nation – to exercise sovereign powers over all the particular states and dynasties. But they had no real assets and no instruments with which to make their will prevail: no army, treasury, civil service, or judiciary. In theory the sinews of power were to be created out of the contributions and contingents supplied by the various states, but these never materialized. It therefore remained to be seen whether moral authority would make up for lack of assets and prove effective enough to compel obedience and respect from parties with different and even contradictory interests.

The Frankfurt Assembly set out to draft a constitution for a state which did not yet exist and about whose shape and character nothing was certain. Paradoxically, its very lack of real power forced the Assembly to stake its claims high, because a small title was not likely to command compliance at all. But in this there was the risk of impotence and ridicule: high claims disregarded bring claimants into contempt.

115, 116
The German National
Assembly at Frankfurt
in 1848. Below,
contemporary cartoon
of one of the deputies
('firm as Germany's
oaks')

The principle of the sovereign power of the nation as a whole
*vis-à-vis* individual German states was not put to the test, and
legislative assemblies in every principality continued to deliberate.
Soon, however, the question of defining the identity and frontiers
of the German nation arose. The Frankfurt liberals and democrats
could not recognize any territorial principle, since this could be
construed as implicitly approving German particularism. They had
to resort to the linguistic criterion. All German-speaking populations,
irrespective of who governed them, were members of the German
nation. For if neither the feudal-dynastic principle nor accident
applied to Hanover, why should it apply to Schleswig and Holstein,
or even to Alsace?

179

Such an attitude was a direct threat to the sovereignty and integrity of neighbouring states. Moreover, it was a double-edged weapon. For it immediately raised the question of the right of the non-German populations under German rule to an independent national status, and of course the thorny and vexatious problem of Austria. The immediate test cases were Schleswig-Holstein and the Polish provinces of Prussia. The Frankfurt Assembly could not well remain indifferent to the call of the Germans who rose against Danish rule. Having no armed force at its disposal, it had to invite the Prussian army to intervene. The King of Prussia had deep qualms about acting as the executive of a national assembly whose title he did not recognize, and against a fellow-king whose title was entirely valid in his eyes. Besides, he was made to feel the strong displeasure of both the Tsar and the British government. After a half-hearted campaign, the Prussians concluded an armistice with the Danes, without the authorization or knowledge of the Frankfurt Assembly. The deputies were filled with impotent rage. Nevertheless, when popular agitation threatened certain Right-wing deputies, the Assembly had no choice but to call in Prussian troops to defend its safety and dignity.

The Polish issue cost German liberalism much of its moral standing. The idea of a war on behalf of Polish independence was soon shelved. *Polenschwärmerei* dwindled to a plan for Polish autonomy within Prussia. As usually happens when national boundaries for territories of mixed population are discussed, no boundary could be agreed. Passions rose to a high pitch. Once mutual hostility was roused, it was natural to invoke requirements of strategy, economic imperatives, and indeed historic claims to negate the abstract principle of national self-determination. The Germans in Posen raised an outcry against being abandoned to an enemy and, moreover, what they considered an inferior race, at the very moment when Germany was making a supreme effort to gather all her children into a common fatherland. Shrill voices were raised in the Assembly against mawkish sentimentality towards nations which, through loss of independence, had proved that they were incapable of defending it, and therefore – in this world of conflict – did not deserve to be free.

'Weltgeschichte war Weltgericht.' It was absurd to try to spread cobwebs of pious principles to stop the flight of eagles. This kind of sentiment was a far cry from liberalism and the idea of reciprocity of rights. The Prussian army squashed the Polish uprising in the province of Posen without difficulty.

The frustrations of the German liberals were aggravated by their fears of the Left. In themselves the stirrings of the masses were of little consequence: peasant unrest in the south, communist demonstrations in the Rhineland, a Jacobin uprising under Hacker and Struve in Baden, some rioting in Berlin and Saxony. The Fourth Estate, which was entirely unrepresented at Frankfurt, made an effort to assert itself, but in a rather innocuous way. The artisans called a Congress to demand a return to the guild system, and in their 'Artisans' Charter' came out against *laissez-faire* policies and the industrial system in general. They demanded a general Chamber for all trades, above the provincial Chambers, on the basis of obligatory membership of corporations and masters' privileges. Workers' representatives under Stephan Born tried with scant success to set up a permanent and all-German Trades Union; a General Congress of Workers met, like the Artisans' Congress, at Frankfurt in the summer of 1848, and decided to set up a Workers' League with the aim of achieving the self-emancipation of the proletariat. The only effective mouthpiece of the socialist revolution was for a while the *Neue Rheinische Zeitung* under the editorship of Karl Marx. At its instigation 234 democratic delegates from 66 towns assembled on 14 June and voiced the demand for a united German Republic based on universal suffrage and radical social policies, and holding out a fraternal hand to all peoples.

Under the impact of the June days in Paris and frustrations at home, the German middle classes, not least the intellectuals, succumbed to the dread of Red anarchy and violence. In comparison with the bloody chaos threatened by mob rule, the ranks of soldiers acting with precision and under strict orders appeared as a guarantee of order and civilization. The army for its part was only too eager to avenge the humiliations it had suffered from the hands of the civilian mob in the days of March.

Such a mood prepared the ground for a recovery by the princes. When the Prussian Landtag showed signs of wishing to control the army, and tried to dismiss officers noted for their devotion to the royal cause, the Prussian King took up the challenge. Here was indeed the supreme test.

The Landtag was dissolved, and the King published a constitution as an act of grace. It offered safeguards for personal liberty and granted universal suffrage, but kept the real levers of power under the King's control: the appointment of a ministry, command over the army, and (as Bismarck demonstrated in the early 1860s) the power to fix the budget and raise taxes without parliamentary approval. After a while universal suffrage was transformed into a three-class system, which gave absolute preponderance to the landowning class. There was to be universal but not equal suffrage.

The March Revolution seemed to sound the death-knell of the Habsburg Empire. Its survival under a régime of popular sovereignty and its concomitant – national self-determination – was possible only on condition of a genuine brotherhood of nations. This indeed was the hope of the radical revolutionaries, like Dr Fischhof, who started the revolution at the University of Vienna, kept it going in the capital, and brought it to its supreme crisis, when the population rose in the autumn of 1848 to stop reinforcements from being sent to crush the Hungarian Revolution.

In the end the monarchy survived triumphant and intact, thanks to the strength of national conflicts within the Empire. Racial strife enabled the Habsburgs to put down every form of secessionist revolt, to prevent the unification of Germany without Austria and under Prussia, and at last even to annul constitutional government within the confines of the Empire and do away with the traditional liberties of the historic provinces.

As a well-calculated gesture towards history and the dynastic tradition, the Frankfurt Assembly appointed a Habsburg archduke as Vicar of the Empire, that is to say as provisional head of the future German Union. But the Assembly decided quite early that it was unthinkable that the roughly fifty per cent of non-Germans in the Austrian Empire should become an integral part of the new united

Germany. As it was not possible to advise the Habsburgs to give up their non-German possessions, and as no one dared to call upon the Austrian Germans to rid themselves of their dynasty and join the future Reich as Germans *tout court*, it was decided that German rulers, members of the new German Empire, could rule over non-German territories only on the basis of personal union. This was a solution which the House of Austria could not accept without undermining its very title to exist and rule.

For many months, however, revolution within the Empire made Austria powerless to assert her will in Germany. Hungary was in flames and, for all practical purposes, independent. There was a successful revolution in Milan, helped by a Piedmontese invasion and volunteers from all over Italy; combined with an uprising in Venice, this had destroyed Austrian rule in the whole of northern Italy. Except for the region of the four fortresses, in which the old Marshal Radetzky was encamped, all the Italian satellites of Austria – the Kingdom of the Two Sicilies, the Papal State, Tuscany, Modena, Parma – were in the throes of revolution. In Prague the Czechs rose to demand a special status for Bohemia, Moravia and Silesia, based partly on historic precedent, partly on abstract national rights. And everywhere else in the vast Danubian Empire unrest was seething: in Galicia and Croatia, among the Rumanians and the Serbs, the Slovenes and the Ukrainians.

In this extremity, the House of Habsburg was saved by the forces which had so long preserved it. The aristocratic generals and the army remained steadfastly faithful. Radetzky struck back, and recovered the whole of Lombardy in one blow. The bombardment of Lemberg and Cracow was enough to stop unrest in Galicia, still shuddering at the nightmare memories of the 1846 *jacquerie*. And Prince Windischgrätz eagerly exploited some minor disturbances in Prague during the Pan-Slav Congress as an excuse to put down the Czech national movement.

The emancipation of the peasants from personal service, coupled with arrangements for redeeming their land, satisfied the long-standing grievances of millions of potentially loyal subjects with no political interests or ambitions of their own. The peasants ceased to be

117, 118 Metternich fleeing from Vienna at the outbreak of the Revolution (left). In Pest, the publication of the 'Twelve Points' meant victory for the Hungarian progressives

a revolutionary class, and in many cases became an effective counter-revolutionary force. For in large parts of the Empire the peasants were not merely an exploited class, but, as stated before, constituted the subject race, while their social masters were the politically and culturally dominant nationality. Slovak, Serb, Croat, Ruthenian and Rumanian serfs had for centuries tilled the soil of Hungarian magnates and gentry; Polish nobles had exploited Ukrainian peasants; and German or Germanized aristocrats lived on the labour of Czechs and other Slavs. There was hardly as yet the counterweight of an industrial proletariat in Austria, except for Vienna and parts of Bohemia.

The rebellious Hungarians continued to be the supreme danger to the Habsburg Empire. Kossuth became the idol of radicals all over the world, and Karl Marx hailed the Hungarian nation as the revolutionary nation *par excellence*. Nevertheless, the Hungarian cause was a very dubious one. Even more than the Germans, the Hungarians promoted the idea of the superiority of historic over unhistoric

119, 120   Barricade in Milan, where a briefly successful revolt was staged; and a Neapolitan *lazzarone*

nations. A small and isolated nation, a latecomer to Europe, wedged in between oceans of Slavs and Germans, with memories of heroic resistance to the Turkish threat, the Magyars were passionately convinced that Hungary must be great, or there would be no Hungary. For a thousand years the Slovaks had lived under Magyar rule, never having had a state of their own, and for centuries Hungarian nobles had ruled the Southern Slavs and the Rumanians. The Hungarians claimed that the subject races should regard themselves – like Bretons in France and Welshmen in Britain – as no more than tribes with dialects of their own. But the 'tribes' of Hungary remained deaf to such persuasions. The argument of the historic nations was that rights to a territory were gained not merely by vegetating on it, but by shaping its civilization. The Germans, the Hungarians, the Poles in Eastern Galicia did this in many of the areas inhabited by other peoples, but dominated by them. Strangely enough, this was also, in a modified form, the argument behind

185

Marx's classification of nations into those which were progressive or revolutionary (such as the Germans, Poles and Hungarians, and of course the great nations of the West) and those which were retrograde, pastoral and from the cultural point of view parasitic (such as the Czechs, the Southern Slavs, the Danes). The former were undergoing industrialization, strove to form larger territorial units and, through their struggle against feudal absolutism, were hastening the day of the Revolution; whereas the latter's very existence helped to postpone it.

The historic nations philosophy was enough to make the unhistoric peoples pause and ask which was their more dangerous enemy – the exclusive and dynamic nationalism of the historic nations, or the easy-going supranational rule of the House of Habsburg. The Habsburgs, after all, did not identify themselves with any race, and were indulgently tolerant of local folk-ways, so long as they carried no rebellious aspirations with them. Indeed, early in the revolution the Emperor's government proclaimed the complete equality of all nationalities and languages.

Paradoxically, it was at the Pan-Slav Congress that the Czech historian Palacky proclaimed that had Austria not existed it would have to be created. The same Palacky caused deep indignation at the Frankfurt Assembly when he refused an invitation to attend, saying: 'I am a Czech, and not a German.' Had not Bohemia and Moravia formed part of the German Empire for centuries, and had not the King of Bohemia been the first Elector?

In these circumstances it was not surprising that the Southern Slavs under Jelačić aided the Austrian troops in the suppression of the Hungarian Revolution. Compromise became impossible, once the Emperor's emissary to Hungary was murdered and the Magyars proclaimed their independence. In a supreme heroic effort Kossuth succeeded in clearing Hungarian territory of Austrian troops. Left with no choice, the new youthful Emperor Francis Joseph applied to the Tsar to save a fellow-monarch from the international revolution. Some weeks later, Paskiewicz, veteran of the suppression of the 1830 Polish uprising (veterans on the other side, incidentally, served as commanders-in-chief of the Hungarian army), was able to

Les trois soutiens de la civilisation austro-croate :
JELLACHICH          RADETZKI          WINDISGRAETZ.

121  French caricature of the 'Three Props of the Austro-Croat civilization':
Jelačić, Radetzky and Windischgrätz, the military leaders who crushed the revolts
in the Austrian Empire

send his master, Nicholas I, the message that 'Hungary lies at Your Majesty's feet.'

The revolution in the Austrian Empire was over. The foolhardy King of Piedmont's army had already been crushed by Radetzky at Novara. Habsburg rule in Italy was fully re-established when, a few days after Hungary's collapse, the heroic defence of Venetia under Daniele Manin came to an end.

Austria's self-confidence was restored, indeed enhanced. Her new leaders – Schwarzenberg, Bach, Bruck, Schmerling and others – were men with no nostalgia for a feudal past and historic traditions; they pursued clear, rational and radical goals, and believed in ruthless centralization and administrative efficiency. Austria took a leaf out of Prussia's book and granted a constitution from above. The Austrian delegates at Frankfurt then vetoed any form of German unity without Austria as an indivisible entity.

Largely depleted by the recall of Austrian deputies and the departure of many Right-wing members, the Frankfurt Assembly could now see only one hope of securing German unity: the assumption of the imperial crown by the King of Prussia over a united Germany, minus Austria. A deputation was sent to wait upon Frederick William IV. He refused to receive 'a crown of mud' from 'master bakers' and 'master butchers' who had no right to offer something which they did not own. A crown could be offered only by crowned heads; in the hierarchy of monarchs none ranked higher than the Habsburg Emperor, and no one had the right to usurp what belonged to him. Thus one type of romanticism was pitted against another.

REALISM TRIUMPHANT

By the summer of 1849 it was all over: the radical rump of the Frankfurt Assembly, chased from pillar to post, melted away, and the feeble and isolated attempts at revolt were easily put down by government troops. The hanging of the Hungarian generals came as a tragic finale to a heroic drama. The Republic of Rome, presided over by Mazzini, was treacherously liquidated by French troops, who were at first thought to have come to save it by rescuing it from the hands of the Austrians. Pope Pius IX returned with a fierce resolve to undo the liberal and revolutionary evils he had helped to unchain as a liberal pope in the first year of his pontificate. The gallant stand of the Roman Republicans, the humane character of the Revolutionary régime and of course the moving story of Garibaldi's escape with his dying wife in his arms, are factors which have cast a romantic light upon the ambivalent fortunes of the Italian Revolution of 1848. The tortuous and insincere King of Sardinia, Charles Albert, who directed or rather misdirected the Revolution, could never make up his mind which he hated and feared more – the Italian Revolution, Austria or the French. He would brace himself to take the plunge usually at the worst moment, with a minimum of preparation and with no power of endurance.

The restored régimes were no longer headed by frightened men with their eyes on the past, endeavouring to do no more than stave off and delay the inevitable day of judgment, but by self-confident

122 Pope Pius IX discards his liberal 'saviour's' mask after the Revolution and reveals his true face when he resumes power in 1849

and determined realists like the new leaders of Austria, who believed they had taken the measure of the adversary and found him not at all redoubtable. Such were Brandenburg, Manteuffel and Bismarck in Prussia, Schwarzenberg and Bach in Austria, and Louis-Napoleon in France.

It was again France that provided the test case. Frightened and bewildered, the French bourgeoisie dreaded the Reds and looked for a saviour: at the same time it wished to retain parliamentary institutions. Few could bring themselves to endorse the brutal consistency and frankness of Romieux, the author of two most significantly titled pamphlets *Spectre rouge* and *L'Ère des Césars*. Romieux jeered at the impotence and confusion of those parliamentary liberals who had first ignited the fuse of revolution and – when the fire started – called in the army. He held that the parliamentary régime lacked the confidence and firmness to resist the barbarian plebs, whose numbers were bound to grow, and who had taken to heart liberal-demo-cratic teachings on the rights to happiness and revolution. Therefore

189

only new Caesars at the head of strong armies could save European civilization and protect the propertied classes. Napoleon III afterwards rewarded Romieux with a directorship of the Beaux-Arts department and the museums of France. It was certainly true that the French bourgeoisie tended to sway between contradictory policies, and as a result was largely ineffectual. In the last analysis, however, it would swing to the forces of order, or at least easily resign itself to the forceful assumption of power by a dictator.

In this respect, a question of vital importance was how to elect a president for the new Republic. In a most eloquent peroration, Lamartine admitted that a president elected by popular vote might be a danger to the parliamentary system in a country torn by class war and party strife. He was therefore the more anxious to give democracy a chance to manifest its strength and the people its good sense and love of liberty. Most of the members who voted for the measure were more interested in securing a strong government. The president was granted all the powers of a head of the executive, with the ministry responsible only to him and the army and the civil service under his command. As if determined to take away with one hand what they had given with the other, the constitution-makers forbade the president or any of his relatives to stand for the presidency again at the end of his four-year term, and also denied him the right to dissolve the Chamber. No provisions were made to resolve a conflict between the legislature and the president. The rules fixed for constitutional revision in effect made any revision impossible because of the timing of the numerous votings and the three-quarter majorities required by the law. Any conflict between the executive and the legislature was therefore bound to issue in total deadlock, or lead to a *coup*. It needed no extraordinary imagination to realize that a Bonaparte president would resort to the latter, especially if the single term restriction was suspended over him like a sword of Damocles.

The election of Louis-Napoleon Bonaparte as President by a crushing majority of 5,500,000 was an event of immense significance. Yesterday's popular hero, Lamartine, received only 17,000 votes; the candidate of the Red Revolution, Raspail, 40,000; the radical

Republican Ledru-Rollin 400,000; and General Cavaignac, famous as the ruthless suppressor of the uprising of the June Days, 1,500,000. Louis-Napoleon was totally unknown to the mass of the nation, had no party machine or funds, was colourless in appearance, and considered harmless by his opponents after his stammering little speech in the Chamber against the law to exclude members of former reigning families from running for the presidency. Because of the magic of his name, he was swept to supreme power by millions of peasants to whom the names of the other candidates meant nothing. He also received votes from the bourgeois praying for order, and of course from the Royalists of both hues – legitimists and Orléanists – who thought the 'excellent young man' of forty (as Thiers called him) would warm the place for a king.

An ominous lesson in the possibilities of mass democracy, and an eye-opener to men like Bismarck and Disraeli. Elected to be the guardian of order, the author of the *Idées Napoléoniennes* saw himself also as the mandatory of the nation in a more real sense than the representatives of partial interests in parliament: as the protector of the poor, as the Saint-Simonist architect of the industrialization of France and chief planner of its economic life and social relationships, as the embodiment of the army – in brief, something for everybody. He gladdens the hearts of the Catholics and the Right by helping the Pope against the Roman Republicans; and then crushes a Red uprising in Paris to protest against this violation of the Constitution, which forbade a French government to rob any nation of its liberty. When the majority in the new Chamber – almost without moderate Republicans, and divided into a massive monarchical Right and a strong Left bloc – takes fright at the election of the Red novelist Eugène Sue to parliament, and by a stroke of the pen disfranchises about a third of the voters, the President solemnly dissociates himself from the anti-democratic action of the parliamentary majority.

The Chamber obstinately refused to revise the Constitution so as to allow Louis-Napoleon to run for a second term. But the bourgeoisie outside the Chamber feared that there would be chaos again in the next year, 1852, when both Napoleon's presidency and the life of the Chamber ended. Bonaparte carried out his *coup* on the anniversary of Austerlitz in the dead of night, with utmost secrecy and according to plans laid down well in advance. Opposition deputies were rounded up, the Chamber was declared dissolved, universal suffrage was restored, and a plebiscite was announced. A most unromantic *coup* from above, in glaring contrast to the Romantic revolution-making of yesterday. 'Better despotism than revolution', proclaimed the Catholic orator, Montalembert. Rather property than liberty, was Marx's interpretation of the way in which the French bourgeoisie handed over its political powers to a dictator.

The same dilemma took a different form in Germany. The fortunes and misfortunes of the Frankfurt Assembly had proved to many liberals that German unity could never be achieved through free consent, but would have to be imposed by force from above. If *Freiheit* and *Einheit* were incompatible, the latter was unhesitatingly to be preferred. A little later Julius Froebel was to write, 'The German nation is sick of principles and doctrines, literary existence and theoretical greatness. What it wants is Power, Power, Power! And whoever gives it power, to him will it give honour, more honour than he can imagine.' And a little earlier the theory of *Realpolitik* was vouchsafed to the Germans in a pamphlet called *Foundations of Political Realism*. It asserted that 'to be sovereign means to exercise power, and only he who possesses power can exercise it. The direct connection between power and sovereignty is the fundamental truth and the key to the whole of history.' In a sense that was also the conclusion drawn by Marx, and he embodied it in his two contradictory statements: the ruthlessly Machiavellian recipe for revolution given in the *Address to the Communist League*, and the famous Preface to his *Introduction to Political Economy*, which lays down that a great social transformation takes place not because it is ethically right or desired by people, but because the conditions have ripened to the point where it must happen. The unification of Germany, Bismarck was to say, would be achieved through blood and iron, and not with the help of persuasive arguments commanding rational or idealistic consent.

Utopian socialism was not the only victim of 1848. The until then axiomatic assumption of a united front of nations struggling for

123, 124   Garibaldi and Count Cavour

liberty against a league of monarchs was tragically disproved, and the close alliance between nationalism and democracy came to an end. Exclusive nationalism asserted itself as incomparably the strongest of all ideologies, ready and able to subordinate everything to its absolute end, the liberty of other nations as well as democracy at home. The monarchs and their allies woke up to the fact that nationalism was not inevitably a revolutionary force, and could indeed be harnessed by them for anti-democratic ends. This was the startling conclusion of Prince Radowitz, the Catholic adviser to the King of Prussia, and the idea behind Frederick William IV's attempt to unite Germany from above by excluding Austria. Austria's humiliation of Prussia at Olmütz, where the older House, with the backing of Russia, simply compelled Prussia to climb down, had a traumatic effect on such Junkers as Bismarck, who a few months earlier had still called the idea of German unity a swindle. What had shortly before seemed an assault on the historic uniqueness of Prussia now took on the aspect of a means of revenging a deep affront and asserting the greatness of Prussia *vis-à-vis* Austria.

The unification of Germany was carried out by Bismarck and the old Prussian army, and not by revolutionary democrats. Cavour, a conservative liberal who exploited international tensions, unified Italy – not Mazzini or Garibaldi, who went into retirement when the goal of his life was achieved.

193

In the second part of the century nationalism became the ally of the Right rather than the Left, except in the case of the unhappy Poles. Satisfied national aspirations, or indeed nationalist wrath (like that of the French after 1870), coupled with growing prosperity and the improved conditions of the working classes, due partly to California gold, partly to the mechanism of self-adjustment which capitalism at its higher stage was able to evolve, had a dampening effect on revolutionary ardour. Such an atmosphere enabled the propertied classes to engage again in more liberal policies. For this, too, foundations had been laid in 1848. In the year of revolutions peasant emancipation was completed everywhere except Russia, and while power was kept by the ruling classes, the basic freedoms – civil rights, equality before the law, trial by jury – were granted to all throughout Europe, although they were much curtailed for the relatively short period of militant reaction.

If we now take a look at the wider world of 1848, two significant and not often remembered facts attract our attention. One was unconnected with the events in Europe, but the other arose directly from the memorable vicissitudes of revolution and counter-revolution. In 1848 the United States of America came into possession of the vast south-western area, and thus brought to fruition the colossal endeavour to turn the whole area from ocean to ocean and from Mexico to Canada into one country. The gold which was soon to be discovered in California and the influx of virile and radical immigrants from Europe, above all political refugees from Germany, were soon – after the terrible upheaval of the Civil War – destined to change a rural economy into the mightiest industrial arsenal of the world.

In 1847 Alexander Herzen came to the West as a refugee. After his experience of the implacable despotism of Nicholas I, who in 1848 even forbade the study of philosophy, Herzen came as a pilgrim, ready to worship the civilization and freedom of the West: 'Paris, the heart of the world, the brain of history, the international bazaar on the Champ-de-Mars, the beginning of the brotherhood of peoples and universal peace.' In the years 1848-9 he experienced a terrible

DEUX UTOPIES.

I.

UNE RUE DE PARIS.

II.

UN DÉSERT ENTRE LA CALIFORNIE ET LE TEXAS.

125  A satire of 1848 demonstrating the futility of two different Utopias, the California gold-rush and the communist Cabet's *Icarie* based on fraternity

revulsion of feeling at the sight of the triumph of bourgeois hypocrisy and pusillanimity, and it was then that he wrote the famous essay, *From the Other Shore*, starting with the words: 'A curse upon you, year of blood and madness, year of the triumph of meanness, beastliness, stupidity! A curse upon you!...'

What did you do, revolutionaries frightened of revolution, political tricksters, buffoons of liberty?...Democracy can create nothing positive....Democrats only know...what they do not want....There is no genuine creation in democracy and therefore it has no future....Socialism left a victor on the field of battle will inevitably be deformed into a commonplace bourgeois philistinism. Then a cry of denial will be wrung from the titanic breast of the revolutionary minority and the deadly battle will begin again....

Beginning with a cry of joy at crossing the frontier, I ended by a spiritual return to my own country. Faith in

195

Russia saved me on the verge of moral ruin. . . . Caesar knew the Gauls better than modern Europe knows the Russians.

At about the same time, the morose Spanish prophet of doom, Donoso Cortés, was warning the world not to think

that the catastrophe will end there. The Slav races in their relationship to the West are not what the Teutons were in their relations with the Roman Empire. . . . From decaying Europe Russia will suck into her pores all the poison with which Europe is already infected. She will herself dissolve from the same decay.

Herzen, joining issue with the apocalyptic reactionary, proclaimed: 'Russia will have its rendezvous with revolution in socialism.'

What effect the great publicist's revulsion of feeling had on those Russians who over the years were to prepare the tremendous cataclysm of 1917 is something no one can tell.

126
Alexander Herzen
(1812–70)

(a) Carr-Saunders's estimate (b) Willcox's estimate

| | 1800 | | 1850 | | 1900 | |
|---|---|---|---|---|---|---|
| | (a) | (b) | (a) | (b) | (a) | (b) |
| Africa | 90 | 100 | 95 | 100 | 120 | 141 |
| North America | 6 | 6 | 26 | 26 | 81 | 81 |
| Latin America | 19 | 23 | 33 | 33 | 63 | 63 |
| Asia | 597 | 595 | 741 | 656 | 915 | 857 |
| Europe and Russia | 192 | 193 | 274 | 274 | 423 | 423 |
| Oceania | 2 | 2 | 2 | 2 | 6 | 6 |
| Total | 906 | 919 | 1171 | 1091 | 1608 | 1571 |

*Percentage distribution*

| | 1800 | | 1850 | | 1900 | |
|---|---|---|---|---|---|---|
| | (a) | (b) | (a) | (b) | (a) | (b) |
| Africa | 9·9 | 10·9 | 8·1 | 9·2 | 7·5 | 9·0 |
| North America | 0·7 | 0·7 | 2·2 | 2·4 | 5·0 | 5·2 |
| Latin America | 2·1 | 2·5 | 2·8 | 3·0 | 3·9 | 4·0 |
| Asia | 65·9 | 64·7 | 63·3 | 60·1 | 56·9 | 54·6 |
| Europe and Russia | 21·2 | 21·0 | 23·1 | 25·1 | 26·3 | 26·9 |
| Oceania | 0·2 | 0·2 | 0·2 | 0·2 | 0·4 | 0·4 |
| Total | 100·0 | 100·0 | 100·0 | 100·0 | 100·0 | 100·0 |

*Annual rate of increase per 1000*

| | 1800–1850 | | 1850–1900 | |
|---|---|---|---|---|
| | (a) | (b) | (a) | (b) |
| Africa | 1·1 | 0·0 | 4·7 | 6·9 |
| North America | 29·8 | 29·8 | 23·0 | 23·0 |
| Latin America | 11·1 | 7·2 | 13·0 | 13·0 |
| Asia | 4·3 | 2·0 | 4·2 | 5·4 |
| Europe and Russia | 7·1 | 7·0 | 8·7 | 8·7 |
| Oceania | — | — | — | — |
| Total | 5·1 | 3·4 | 6·4 | 7·3 |

(From the *Cambridge Economic History of Europe*, v. VI, p. 58)

| | BELGIUM | FRANCE | U.K. | ITALY | GERMANY | RUSSIA (unreliable) |
|---|---|---|---|---|---|---|
| *1800* | 3·0 | 26·9 | (*1811*) 18·1 | 18·5 | 24·5 | (*1811*) 44 |
| *1850* | 4·3 (*1846*) | 36·5* | 22·3 | 23·9* | 31·7* | (*1859*) 58·6* |

★ Indicates a boundary change since the previous figure.
(From the *Cambridge Economic History of Europe*, v. VI, pp. 61, 63.) The figure for U.K. in 1811 taken from D. Thomson, *Europe since Napoleon*, London 1957, p. 94. The figures for Germany seem to refer to present-day frontiers. F. Lütge gives the respective figures: 1800 – 24·4, 1850 – 35·4. (Friedrich Lütge, *Deutsche Sozial- und Wirtschaftsgeschichte*, Berlin 1952, p. 306)

| | Paris |
|---|---|
| *1801* | 546,856 |
| *1846* | 1,053,900 |

The growth of small industrial towns is manifested by the following figures:

| | Roubaix | Saint Etienne | Mulhouse |
|---|---|---|---|
| *1812* | — | — | 10,000 |
| *1827* | 8,000 | 16,000 | 20,000 |
| *1836* | 34,000 | 54,000 | 30,000 |

(From J. H. Clapham, *Economic Development of France and Germany*, Cambridge 1961, pp. 53, 54 and J. L. Talmon, *Political Messianism*, London 1960, pp. 340–1)

ENGLAND

| | London | Glasgow | Birmingham | Manchester |
|---|---|---|---|---|
| *1815* | 988,000 | 77,000 | 71,000 | 95,000 |
| *1848* | 2,363,000 | 329,000 | 232,000 | 401,000 |

(From Robert Schnerb, *Le XIX^e siècle, l'Apogée de l'expansion européenne 1815–1914,* Histoire Générale des Civilisations, VI, Paris 1957, p. 47)


PERCENTAGE OF
THE POPULATION
LIVING IN TOWNS

| | | ENGLAND | FRANCE |
|---|---|---|---|
| *1815* | (in towns above 5,000) · | 28% | 14% |
| *1870* | (in towns above 10,000) | 57% | 21% |

(From the *Propyläen Weltgeschichte*, VIII, p. 303)


RURAL
POPULATION
IN PRUSSIA

| | |
|---|---|
| *1816* | 73·5% |
| *1846* | 72·0% |
| *1852* | 71·5% |

(From J. H. Clapham, *op. cit.*, p. 82)


GROWTH OF TRADE

*Clearances at United Kingdom Ports (average a year)*

| | 1821–1830 | 1861–1870 |
|---|---|---|
| British vessels | 1,782,000 tons | 10,122,000 tons |
| Foreign vessels | 662,000 tons | 5,276,000 tons |


*British Annual Averages of Exports (value in £)*

| | 1822–1830 | 1862–1870 |
|---|---|---|
| iron and steel | £1,046,000 | £16,213,000 |
| | 1827–1830 | 1867–1870 |
| machinery and millwork | £232,000 | £5,028,000 |


*Totals of Exports and Imports*

| | 1801 | 1848 |
|---|---|---|
| France | £28,700,000 | £65,700,000 |
| Britain | £66,900,000 | £295,800,000 |

(Figures from W. Bowden, M. Karporich, A. P. Usher, *An Economic History of Europe since 1750*, N.Y. 1937, pp. 408, 409, 447)


*Output of Iron (in tons)*

| | 1830 | 1850 |
|---|---|---|
| U.K. | 680,000 | 2,250,000 |
| France | 270,000 | 400,000 |
| Germany | 46,000★ | 215,000 |
| U.S.A. | 180,000 | 560,000 |
| World | 1,600,000 | 4,470,000 |

(From the *New Cambridge Modern History*, v. X, p. 29)
★ Jürgen Kuczynski, *Die Geschichte der Lage der Arbeiter in England seit 1832*, Berlin 1955, p. 17, gives the figure 120,000 for Germany in 1830.


*Railways*

Kilometers of Railways in Operation by the *End of 1850*

| | | | |
|---|---|---|---|
| Belgium | 900 | Spain | 28 |
| France | 3,000 | Holland | 176 |
| Germany (1871 area) | 6,000 | Switzerland | 25 |
| Italy | 400 | United Kingdom | 10,500 |

(From J. H. Clapham, *op. cit.*, p. 339)

*Mercantile Tonnage of All Kinds on National Register*

|  | *1840* | *1850* |
|---|---|---|
| United Kingdom | 2,768,000 | 3,565,000 |
| United States (foreign trade) | 900,000 | 1,586,000 |
| France | 662,500 | 688,000 |
| Norway | 277,000 | 298,000 |
| Holland | — | 293,000 |
| Hamburg | — | 71,000 |
| Bremen | 44,000 | 68,000 |
| Belgium | 23,000 | 35,000 |

(From J. H. Clapham, *op. cit.*, p. 112)

*Capacity of All Steam-Engines (in thousands of horse-power)*

|  | *1840* | *1850* |  | *1840* | *1850* |
|---|---|---|---|---|---|
| Great Britain | 620 | 1,290 | Russia | 20 | 70 |
| Germany | 40 | 260 | Italy | 10 | 40 |
| France | 90 | 270 | U.S.A. | 760 | 1,680 |
| Austria | 20 | 100 | Europe | 860 | 2,240 |
| Belgium | 40 | 70 | World | 1,650 | 3,990 |

From the *Cambridge Economic History of Europe*, v. VI, p. 449)

*Output of Coal (in tons)*

|  | *1800* | *1840* | *1850* |
|---|---|---|---|
| England | 10,000,000 | 30,000,000 | 49,000,000 |
| Germany | 300,000 | 3,400,000 | 6,700,000 |
| France | 800,000 | 3,000,000 | 4,400,000 |

(Figures of Jürgen Kuczynski, quoted by Jacques Droz, *Les révolutions allemandes de 1848*, Paris 1957, p. 73)

*The Value of Global Industrial Production (in millions £)*

|  | *1800* | *1820* | *1840* |
|---|---|---|---|
| Germany | 60 | 85 | 150 |
| England | 230 | 290 | 387 |
| France | 190 | 220 | 264 |
| U.S.A. | 25 | 55 | 96 |

(From Jürgen Kuczynski, *Die Geschichte der Lage der Arbeiter in Deutschland von 1800 bis in die Gegenwart*, Berlin 1946, I, p. 17)

*Consumption of Raw Cotton (in metric tons)*

|  | *1815* | *1832* | *1850* |
|---|---|---|---|
| England | 36,932 | 125,634 | 222,046 |
| France |  | 33,623 | 59,273 |
| Belgium |  | 2,435 | 7,222 |
| The 'Zollverein' |  | 2,422 | 17,117 |

(From the *Cambridge Economic History of Europe*, v. VI, p. 394)

*Cotton Spindlage (in thousands)*

|  | *1834* | *1850* |
|---|---|---|
| Britain | 10,000 | 18,000 |
| U.S.A. | 1,400 | 5,500 |
| France | 2,500 | 4,500 |
| Germany (*1836*) | 626 | 900 |

(From the *Cambridge Economic History of Europe*, v. VI, p. 443)

# SELECTED BIBLIOGRAPHY

## RECENT WORKS OF GENERAL SYNTHESIS

*The New Cambridge Modern History*
v. IX: *War and Peace in an Age of Upheaval, 1793–1830* (Cambridge 1965)
v. X: *The Zenith of European Power, 1830–1870* (Cambridge 1960)
*Historia Mundi*
10. Band: *Das 19. und 20. Jahrhundert* (Bern and Munich 1961)
*Propyläen Weltgeschichte*
VIII. Band: *Das neunzehnte Jahrhundert* (Berlin, etc. 1960)

Jacques Droz et al.     *Restaurations et révolutions (1815–1871)* ('Clio', v. 9, Paris 1953)

E. J. Hobsbawm     *The Age of Revolution, Europe 1789–1848* (London 1962)

Lefebvre, Georges     *La révolution française* (Peuples et civilisations, v. XIII, Paris 1963)
*Napoléon* (Peuples et civilisations, v. XIV, Paris 1941)

Félix Ponteil     *L'Éveil des nationalités et le mouvement libéral (1815–48)* (Peuples et civilisations, v. XV, Paris 1960)

Charles-H. Pouthas     *Démocraties et capitalisme (1848–60)* (Peuples et civilisations, v. XVI, Paris 1941)

Robert Schnerb     *Le XIXᵉ siècle—l'Apogée de l'expansion européenne, 1815–1914* (Histoire générale des civilisations, VI, Paris 1957)

David Thomson     *Europe since Napoleon* (London 1964: Penguin ed., London 1966)

## NATIONAL HISTORIES

AUSTRIA
Heinrich Ritter von Srbik     *Metternich: der Staatsmann und der Mensch*, 3 vols. (Munich 1954–7)

ENGLAND
Asa Briggs     *The Age of Improvement, 1783–1867* (London 1959)
Elie Halévy     *A History of the English People in the Nineteenth Century*, trans. E. I. Watkin, 6 vols. (London 1949–52)
E. L. Woodward     *The Age of Reform, 1815–70* (Oxford 1938)

FRANCE
G. Bertier de Savigny     *La restauration* (Paris 1952)
S. Charléty     *La restauration* and *La monarchie de juillet* (1830–48), being vols. V and VI of *Histoire de France contemporaine*, ed. Ernest Lavisse (Paris 1921)
P. Thureau-Dangin     *Histoire de la monarchie de juillet*, 7 vols. (Paris 1884–92)

GERMANY
Geoffrey Barraclough     *The Origins of Modern Germany* (Oxford 1949)
Werner Conze (ed.)     *Staat und Gesellschaft im deutschen Vormärz 1815–1848* (Sieben Beiträge von Theodor Schieder et al., Stuttgart 1962)

Koppel Shub Pinson      *Modern Germany: Its History and Civilization* (New York
                        1959)
Franz Schnabel          *Deutsche Geschichte im neunzehnten Jahrhundert*, 4 vols.
                        (Freiburg i. Breisgau 1947–51)
A.J.P.Taylor            *The Course of German History* (London 1951)

ITALY
G.F.H.Berkeley          *Italy in the Making*, 2 vols. (Cambridge 1932–40)
A.J.Whyte               *The Evolution of Modern Italy* (Oxford 1944)

RUSSIA
J.D.Clarkson            *A History of Russia* (London 1962)
Michael T. Florinsky    *Russia, A History and an Interpretation* v. II (New York 1961)

ECONOMIC HISTORY

                        *The Cambridge Economic History of Europe* v. VI: *The
                        Industrial Revolution and After* (Cambridge 1965)
T.S.Ashton              *The Industrial Revolution, 1760–1830* (London 1949)
J.H.Clapham             *Economic Development of France and Germany, 1815–1914*
                        (Cambridge 1961)
William Henry           *A Concise Economic History of Britain from 1750 to Recent
  Bassano Court         Times* (Cambridge 1954)
Arthur Louis            *The Industrial Revolution in France, 1815–48* (New York
  Dunham                1955)
Pauline Gregg           *A Social and Economic History of Britain, 1760–1950* (London
                        1950)
Herbert Heaton          *Economic History of Europe* (New York 1948)
W. Bowden,              *An Economic History of Europe since 1750* (New York 1937)
M. Karpovich and
A.P.Usher
Jürgen Kuczynski        *Die Geschichte der Lage der Arbeiter in England seit 1832*
                        (Berlin 1955)
                        *Die Geschichte der Lage der Arbeiter in Deutschland von 1800
                        bis in die Gegenwart*, Band I: 1800 bis 1932 (Berlin 1946)
                        *Labour Conditions in Western Europe, 1820 to 1935* (New
                        York 1936)
E.Labrousse (ed.)       *Aspects de la crise et de la dépression de l'économie française au
                        milieu du XIXᵉ siècle* (Etudes . . . Bibliothèque de la révolu-
                        tion de 1848, Paris 1956)
                        *Le mouvement ouvrier et les idées sociales* (Les Cours de
                        Sorbonne, Centre de Documentation universitaire, Paris
                        1948)
                        *Comment naissent les révolutions* (Acte du Centenaire de 1848,
                        Paris 1948)
                        *Aspects de l'évolution économique et sociale de la France et du
                        Royaume Uni de 1815 à 1890* (Centre de Documentation
                        universitaire, Paris 1948)
Friedrich Lütge         *Deutsche Sozial- und Wirtschaftsgeschichte* (Berlin 1952)
Henri E. Sée            *La vie économique de la France sous la monarchie censitaire,
                        1815–1848* (Paris 1927)

# THE GRAND DEBATE

*Original works*

|---|---|
| Jeremy Bentham | *An Introduction to the Principles of Morals and Legislation* (New York 1961) |
| J.M.Bonald | *Oeuvres complètes*, ed. Migne (Paris 1859) |
| | *Théorie du pouvoir politiques et religieux dans la société*, 3 vols. (Paris 1834) |
| Edmund Burke | *The Works of Edmund Burke*, 9 vols. (London 1891–1911) |
| | *Extraits*, ed. Paul Bourget and Michael Salomon (Paris 1904) |
| Benjamin Constant | *Cours de politique constitutionnelle*, ed. Laboulaye, 2 vols. (Paris 1861) |
| | *Oeuvres politiques*, ed. Ch. Louandre (Paris 1874) |
| François Guizot | *Mémoires pour servir à l'histoire de mon temps*, 8 vols. (Paris 1858–67) |
| | *Of Democracy in Modern Societies* (London 1838) |
| | *Democracy in France* (London 1849) |
| Wilhelm von Humboldt | *Über die Grenzen der Wirksamkeit des Staates* (Nuremberg 1946) |
| Alphonse Lamartine | *La politique de Lamartine* (Choix de discours et écrits politiques, ed. Rouchaud) 2 vols. (Paris 1878) |
| | *La France parlementaire, 1834–1851* (Oeuvres oratoires et écrits politiques) 16 vols. (Paris 1864) |
| H.F.(Robert de) Lamennais | *Oeuvres complètes*, 10 vols. (Paris 1844) |
| | *Lettres inédites à Montalembert*, ed. Forgues (Paris 1898) |
| J.S.Mill | *Mill on Bentham and Coleridge*, ed. F.R.Leavis (London 1950) |
| Adam Müller | *Die Elemente der Staatskunst* (Leipzig 1936) |
| Joseph de Maistre | *Considérations sur la France*, intro. by René Johannet and François Vermale (Paris 1936) |
| | *Les soirées de Saint-Pétersbourg:* Extraits, Traité sur les sacrifices (Paris 1911) |
| | *Du pape* (Lyon 1873) |
| | *Une politique expérimentale* (Introduction et textes choisis par Bernard de Vaulx, Paris 1940) |
| | *Étude sur la souveraineté* (Oeuvres complètes, v. I, Lyon 1884) |
| | *Essai sur le principe générateur des constitutions politiques* (Oeuvres complètes, v. I, Lyon 1884) |
| Adam Smith | *An Inquiry into the Nature and Causes of the Wealth of Nations*, ed. Edwin Cannan, 2 vols. (London 1961) |
| Alexis de Tocqueville | *Oeuvres complètes*, 9 vols. (Paris 1864–6) |
| | *Recollections*, ed. J.P.Mayer (London 1848) |

*Studies*

| | |
|---|---|
| G. Bertier de Savigny | *Metternich and His Times* (London 1962) |
| D. Baggé | *Les idées politiques en France sous la restauration* (Paris 1952) |
| Werner Conze (ed.) | *Op. cit.* |
| Jacques Droz | *L'Allemagne et la révolution française* (Paris 1949) |
| K. Griewank | *Der neuzeitliche Revolutionsbegriff: Entstehung und Entwicklung* (Weimar 1955) |
| Elie Halévy | *The Growth of Philosophical Radicalism*, trans. M. Morris (Boston 1955) |

| | |
|---|---|
| Maxime Leroy | *Histoire des idées sociales en France*, v. II (Paris 1950) |
| Karl Mannheim | *Essays on Sociology and Social Psychology*, Chapter II: 'Conservative Thought' (London 1953) |
| Ch. Morazé | *La France bourgeoise: XVIII^e–XX^e siècles* (Paris 1946) |
| John Plamenatz | *The Revolutionary Movement in France (1815–1871)* (London 1952) |
| Friedrich C. Sell | *Die Tragödie des deutschen Liberalismus* (Stuttgart 1953) |
| J.L. Talmon | *Political Messianism, the Romantic Phase* (London 1960) |
| J. Tchernoff | *Le parti républicain sous la monarchie de juillet* (Paris 1901) |
| E. L. Woodward | *Three Studies in European Conservatism* (London 1929) |

# SOCIALISM

*Original works*

| | |
|---|---|
| Johann Gottlieb Fichte | *Sämtliche Werke*, 8 vols. (Berlin 1845–6) |
| | *Nachgelassene Werke*, 3 vols. (Bonn 1834–5) |
| Charles Fourier | *Oeuvres complètes*, 6 vols. (Paris 1841–5) |
| | *Manuscrits de Charles Fourier*, 2 vols. (Paris 1903) |
| | *Le socialisme sociétaire*, Extraits des œuvres complètes, ed. Hubert Bourgin (Paris 1903) |
| | *Selections from the Works of Fourier*, ed. Charles Gide (London 1901) |
| G. W. F. Hegel | *Early Theological Writings*, trans. T. M. Knox, intro. by R. Kroner (Chicago 1948) |
| | *The Phenomenology of the Spirit*, trans. J. B. Baillie (London 1931) |
| | *Philosophy of Right*, trans. T. M. Knox (Oxford 1942) |
| | *Philosophy of History* (in *The Philosophy of Hegel*, ed. Carl J. Friedrich, New York 1953) |
| Immanuel Kant | *Werke*, ed. Ernst Cassirer, 10 vols. and Ergänzungsband (Berlin 1912–18) |
| | *The Philosophy of Kant*, ed. Carl J. Friedrich (New York 1950) |
| Karl Marx | *Die Frühschriften*, ed. Siegfried Landschut (Stuttgart 1953) |
| Karl Marx and Friedrich Engels | *Historische-kritische Gesamtausgabe: Werke, Schriften, Briefe* (Moscow 1927–35) |
| Robert Owen | *A New View of Society and other writings* (London 1927) |
| Pierre Joseph Proudhon | *Qu'est-ce que la propriété? ou Recherches sur le principe du droit et du gouvernement* (Paris 1840–41) |
| Henri, Comte de Saint-Simon | *Oeuvres*, ed. Rodrigues (Paris 1841) |
| | *Oeuvres choisies*, 3 vols. (Bruxelles 1959) |
| | *Selected Writings*, ed. and trans. F. M. H. Markham (Oxford 1952) |
| | *Exposition de la doctrine de Saint-Simon*, two editions, ed. and intro. by Bouglé and Valévy (Paris 1830 and 1924) |
| —— (et Enfantin) | *Oeuvres*, 47 vols. (Paris 1865–78) |

*Studies*

| | |
|---|---|
| Max Beer | *A History of British Socialism* (London 1953) |
| Celestin Bouglé | *Socialisme française du 'socialisme utopique' à la 'démocratie industrielle'* (Paris 1933) |
| | *Chez les prophètes socialistes, l'alliance intellectuelle franco-allemande* (Paris 1918) |

203

| | |
|---|---|
| Hubert Bourgin | *Fourier, Contribution à l'étude du socialisme français* (Paris 1905) |
| Ernst Cassirer | *Kants Leben und Werke* (Berlin 1913) |
| S. Charléty | *Histoire du Saint-Simonisme* (Paris 1931) |
| G.D.H.Cole | *A History of Socialist Thought*, v. I: *The Forerunners, 1779–1850* (London 1955) |
| | *A Short History of the British Working Class Movement, 1787–1947* (London 1948) |
| A.Cornu | *Karl Marx und Friedrich Engels, Leben und Werke*, Band I: 1818–1844 (Berlin 1954) |
| Wilhelm Dilthey | *Die Jugendgeschichte Hegels* (Berlin 1905) |
| Edouard Dolléans | *Histoire du mouvement ouvrier*, v. I: 1830–71 (Paris 1948) |
| David Owen Evans | *Le socialisme romantique: Pierre Leroux et ses contemporains* (Paris 1948) |
| Charles Gide and Charles Rist | *A History of Economic Doctrines* (London 1915) |
| Elie Halévy | *Histoire du socialisme européen* (Paris 1948) |
| Sidney Hook | *From Hegel to Marx* (London 1936) |
| George G. Iggers | *The Cult of Authority, the Political Philosophy of the Saint-Simonians* (The Hague 1958) |
| Maxime Leroy | *Le socialisme des producteurs. Henri de Saint-Simon* (Paris 1924) |
| George Lichtheim | *Marxism* (London 1964) |
| G.Lukács | *Der junge Hegel* (Berlin 1945) |
| | 'Zur philosophischen Entwicklung des jungen Marx', *Deutsche Zeitschrift für Philosophie*, 2. Jahrgang (Berlin 1954) pp. 288–344 |
| Frank E. Manuel | *The New World of Henry Saint-Simon* (Cambridge, Mass. 1956) |
| H.Marcuse | *Reason and Revolution, Hegel and the Rise of Social Theory* (London and New York 1941) |
| Gustav Mayer | *Friedrich Engels*, 2 vols. (The Hague 1934) |
| Thilo Ramm | *Die grossen Sozialisten als Rechts- und Sozialphilosophen*, v. I (Stuttgart 1955) |
| Frank Ferdinand Rosenblatt | *The Chartist Movement in its Social and Economic Aspects* (New York 1916) |
| Maximilien Rubel | *Karl Marx, Essai de philosophie intellectuelle* (Paris 1957) |
| J.L.Talmon | *Op. cit.* |
| Werner Stark | *The Ideal Foundations of Economic Thought, Three Essays on the Philosophy of Economics* (London 1944) |
| Sidney and Beatrice Webb | *The History of Trade Unionism* (London 1950) |

## NATIONALISM

*Original works*

| | |
|---|---|
| J.C.Fichte | *Addresses to the German Nation*, trans. R.F.Jones and G.H. Thurnbull (Chicago and London 1922) |
| J.G.Herder | *Sämtliche Werke*, ed. B. Suphan (Berlin 1877–1913) |
| Giuseppe Mazzini | *Scritti editi ed inediti*, 94 vols. (Imola 1906–43) |
| | *Life and Writings*, 6 vols. (London 1864–70) |
| | *Essays*, trans. Okey, ed. Bolton King (London 1894) |

| | |
|---|---|
| | *Selected Essays*, ed. W. Clarke (London 1886) |
| | *Selected Writings*, ed. N. Gangulee (London 1945) |
| | *The Duties of Man and other essays*, introd. Thomas Jones (London 1945) |
| Jules Michelet | *Introduction à l'histoire universelle* (Paris 1834) |
| | *Le peuple* (Paris 1846) |
| | *Histoire de la révolution française* (Paris 1847...) |
| Adam Mickiewicz | *Ksiegi narodu i pielgrzymstwa polskiego*, ed. Pigon (London 1941) |
| | *Les slaves*, Cours professé au Collège de France, 1840–41, 5 vols. (Paris 1849) |

*Studies*

| | |
|---|---|
| Georges Bourgin | *La Formation de l'unité italienne* (Paris 1948) |
| Pieter Geyl | *Debates with Historians* (London 1955) |
| Carlton J. Hayes | *The Historical Evolution of Modern Nationalism* (New York 1951) |
| Rudolf Haym | *Herder*, 2 vols. (Berlin 1958) |
| Robert A. Kann | *The Multinational Empire, Nationalism and National Reform in the Habsburg Monarchy, 1848–1918*, 2 vols. (New York 1964) |
| Elie Kedourie | *Nationalism* (London 1961) |
| Bolton King | *A History of Italian Unity* (London 1934) |
| Hans Kohn | *The Idea of Nationalism, A Study in Its Origins and Background* (New York 1951) |
| | *Prophets and Peoples* (New York 1946) |
| Manfred Kridl | *Mickiewicz i Lamennais* (Warsaw 1909) |
| Friedrich Meinecke | *Weltbürgertum und Nationalstaat* (Munich 1962) |
| Charles-H. Pouthas | *Les problèmes des nationalités dans la première moitié du XIXᵉ siècle* (Les Cours de Sorbonne, Paris 1950) |
| G. Salvemini | *Mazzini* (London 1956) |
| Boyd C. Schafer | *Nationalism: Myth and Reality* (New York 1955) |
| R. W. Seton-Watson | *A History of Czechs and Slovaks* (London 1943) |
| Heinrich Ritter von Srbik | *Deutsche Einheit: Idee und Wirklichkeit vom Heiligen Reich bis Königgrätz*, 2 vols. (Munich 1940) |
| J. L. Talmon | *Op. cit.* |
| | *The Unique and the Universal* (London 1965, New York 1966) |
| J. Ujejski | *Wieley Poeci 1848 roku* (Warsaw 1925) |
| Otto Vossler | *Mazzinis politisches Denken und Wollen in den geistigen Strömungen seiner Zeit* (Munich 1927) |
| Georges Weill | *L'Europe du XIXᵉ siècle et l'idée de nationalité* (Paris 1935) |

# ROMANTICISM

ENGLAND

*Original works*

| | |
|---|---|
| William Blake | *The Complete Writings*, ed. G. Keynes (London 1957) |
| Lord Byron | *The Poetical Works* (London and Oxford 1957) |
| | *Selected Poetry and Letters*, ed. Edward E. Bostetter (New York 1961) |

| | |
|---|---|
| S.T.Coleridge | *Select Poetry and Prose*, ed. S. Potter (London 1933)<br>*The Complete Poetical Works*, with notes by E.H.Coleridge (Oxford 1912)<br>*Inquiring Spirit:* a new presentation of Coleridge from his published and unpublished prose writings, ed. K.Coburn (London 1951) |
| Percy Bysshe Shelley | *The Complete Poetical Works*, ed. T.Hutchinson (London and Oxford 1956)<br>*Selected Poetry and Prose*, ed. K.N.Cameron (New York 1960) |
| William Wordsworth | *The Poetical Works*, ed. T.Hutchinson (London and Oxford 1928) |
| *Studies*<br>Meyer Howard Abrams | *The Mirror and the Lamp; Romantic Theory and the Critical Tradition* (New York 1953) |
| Louis Cazamian and Emile Legouis | *A Short History of English Literature* (London 1931) |
| Graham Goulden Hough | *The Romantic Poets* (London 1960) |
| Basil Willey | *The Eighteenth Century Background* (Harmondsworth 1962)<br>*Nineteenth Century Studies: Coleridge to Matthew Arnold* (Harmondsworth 1964) |

# FRANCE

| | |
|---|---|
| *Original works*<br>F.A.R.Vicomte de Châteaubriand | *Mémoires*, présenté par Claude Roy (Paris 1964) |
| Victor Hugo | *Témoin de son siècle*, présentation de Claude Roy (Paris 1962) |
| Lamartine | *Méditations poétiques*, intro. by Jean des Cognets (Paris 1950)<br>*Recueillements poétiques*, intro. by Jean des Cognets (Paris 1925) |
| Alfred de Musset | *La confession d'un enfant du siècle*, intro. and notes by Maurice Allem (Paris 1956) |
| *Studies*<br>Pierre Moreau | *Le romantisme* (Paris 1957) |
| G.Lanson | *Histoire de la littérature française* (Paris 1963) |
| Paul van Tieghem | *Le romantisme dans la littérature européenne* (Paris 1948) |

# GERMANY

| | |
|---|---|
| *Original works* | *Romanticism: Kleist, Novalis, Tieck, Schlegel*, ed. and annotated by Max Dufner and Valentine C. Hubbs (New York 1964)<br>*Sturm und Drang*, kritische Schriften, ed. E. Loewenthal (Heidelberg 1949) |
| Novalis | *Gesammelte Werke*, ed. Carl Seelig, 5 vols. (Herrliberg–Zürich 1945)<br>*Auswahl und Einleitung* von Walther Rehua (Frankfurt 1956) |
| August Wilhelm Schlegel | *Kritische Schriften*, selected by Emile Staiger (Zürich 1962)<br>*Lectures on Dramatic Art and Literature*, trans. John Black, ed. A.J.W.Morrison (London 1886) |

| | |
|---|---|
| Friedrich Schlegel | *Kritische Schriften*, Teilsammlung (Munich 1956)<br>*Schriften und Fragmente, ein Gesamtbild seines Geistes*, compiled and introduced by Ernst Behler (Stuttgart 1956)<br>*Lectures on the History of Literature, Ancient and Modern* (London 1871) |

*Studies*

| | |
|---|---|
| Richard Benz | *Die deutsche Romantik, Geschichte einer geistigen Bewegung* (Leipzig 1937) |
| Henry Brunschwig | *La crise de l'état prussien à la fin du XVIIIe siècle et la genèse de la mentalité romantique* (Paris 1947) |
| Jacques Droz | *Le romantisme politique en Allemagne* (Paris 1963) |
| Rudolf Haym | *Op. cit.* |
| Ricarda Huch | *Die Romantik*, 2 vols. (Leipzig 1920) |
| Paul Kluckhohn | *Das Ideengut der deutschen Romantik* (Handbücherei der Deutschkunde, Band 8, Tübingen 1961) |
| Hermann August Korff | *Geist der Goethezeit: Versuch einer ideellen Entwicklung der klassisch-romantischen Literaturgeschichte*, 5 vols. (Leipzig 1949–57) |
| Arthur O. Lovejoy | *Essays in the History of Ideas* (New York 1960) |
| Oskar Walzel | *Deutsche Romantik* (Leipzig 1923) |

ART AND MUSIC

| | |
|---|---|
| Marcel Brion | *Romantic Art* (London 1960) |
| Donald Jay Grout | *A History of Western Music* (New York) 1960 |
| Louis Hautecoeur *et al.* | *Le romantisme et l'art*, preface by E. Herriot (Paris 1928) |
| Eugénie de Keyser | *The Romantic West, 1789–1850* (Geneva 1965) |
| Wilfred Mellers | *Romanticism and the Twentieth Century* (Man and His Music, v. IV, London 1957) |
| Eric Newton | *The Romantic Rebellion* (London 1962) |

1848 AND AFTER

| | |
|---|---|
| Albert Crémieux | *La révolution de février*, étude critique sur les journées des 21, 22, 23, et 24 février 1848 (Paris 1912) |
| Jacques Droz | *Les révolutions allemandes de 1848* (Paris 1957) |
| François Fejto (ed.) | *The Opening of an Era—1848*, An Historical Symposium, intro. by A.J.P.Taylor (London 1948) |
| P. de la Gorce | *Histoire de la Seconde République Française*, v. I–II (Paris 1925) |
| Albert Guérard | *Napoleon III* (Cambridge, Mass. 1943) |
| Henri Guillemin | *La tragédie de quarante-huit* (Paris 1948) |
| C. Donald Mackay | *The National Workshops* (Cambridge, Mass. 1933) |
| Louis B. Namier | *1848: The Revolution of the Intellectuals* (London 1944) |
| Priscilla Robertson | *Revolutions of 1848: A Social History* (Princeton 1952) |
| Charles Schmidt | *Des ateliers nationaux aux barricades de juin* (Paris 1948) |
| F.A.Simpson | *The Rise of Louis Napoleon* (London 1950)<br>*Louis Napoleon and the Recovery of France* (London 1951) |
| Rudolph Stadlemann | *Soziale und Politische Geschichte der Revolution von 1848* (Munich 1948) |
| Veit Valentin | *Geschichte der deutschen Revolution von 1848–49* (Berlin 1930–31) |

# LIST OF ILLUSTRATIONS

1 The revolutionary association. Caricature by R. Cruikshank, 1821. British Museum, London. Photo: Freeman

2 Feast of the Supreme Being. Anon. colour print, 1790. Musée Carnavalet, Paris. Photo: Foliot

3 The opening of the Canterbury–Whitstable Railway. Colour lithograph, 1830. The Science Museum, London

4 Map of Europe in 1815

5 The Vienna Congress. Anon. French cartoon, 1815. Photo: Freeman

6 The Vienna Congress. Sketch by Isabey, 1815. Louvre, Paris. Photo: Archives Photographiques

7 Iron Foundry at Neustadt–Eberswalde. Oil on panel by Carl Blechen, c. 1832. National-galerie, Berlin

8 The Yorkshire Collier. Engraving after a watercolour by G. Walker, 1814. British Museum, London. Photo: Freeman

9 Le Français d'autrefois. Cartoon, c. 1791. Bibliothèque Nationale, Paris. Photo: Foliot

10 Le Français d'aujourd'hui. Cartoon, c. 1791. Bibliothèque Nationale, Paris. Photo: Foliot

11 Allegory of the Concordat of 1802. Painting by François, 1802. Private Collection of M. Theys, Paris. Photo: Bulloz

12 Fête de la Fédération. Popular painting, 1790. Musée Carnavalet, Paris

13 Evening Prayer. Lithograph after a drawing by E. Lami from his Voyage en Angleterre, 1829. British Museum, London. Photo: Freeman

14 Bible-reader in a Night Refuge. Etching by Gustave Doré from London, 1872. British Museum, London. Photo: Freeman

15 Louis XVIII in his study; painting by F. Gérard, 1823. Musée de Versailles. Photo: Giraudon

16 The memorable events of the French Revolution, 20 June 1789–1800. Popular cartoon. Bibliothèque Nationale, Paris

17 The Freedom of the Press. Lithograph by Honoré Daumier. Rosenwald Collection, National Gallery of Art, Washington D.C.

18 Paris cobbler. Drawing from Leipziger Illustrierte Zeitung, 1845. British Museum, London. Photo: Freeman

19 The politician's breakfast or the devourer of newspapers. Anon. French cartoon, 1815. Photo: Brompton Studio

20 The censor on his hobby-horse. Detail of Le Charenton Ministériel, lithograph by Daumier from La Caricature, No. 83, 1832. British Museum, London

21 French medal commemorating the Polish rebellion, 1830. British Museum, London. Photo: Freeman

22 French Caunois medal commemorating the events of 31 July 1830. British Museum, London. Photo: Freeman

23 Students' Wartburg festival. Anon. drawing, 1817. Photo: Ullstein

24 The Insurgent Grocer. Lithograph by Honoré Daumier, 1830. British Museum, London. Photo: Freeman

25 Liberty Leading the People. Painting by Eugène Delacroix, 1830. Louvre, Paris.

26 Charles X. French medal, 1827. British Museum, London. Photo: Freeman

27 Satire on the parvenu society of the Directoire. Caricature by Isabey, 1798. Photo: Brompton Studio

28 'Corpse Head' of Napoleon. English edition of a German satire by Voltz, 1814. British Museum, London. Photo: Freeman

29 Napoleon. Medal by Pierre-Jean David d'Angers. Musée P.J.David, Angers

30 The Last Scene of the Triumph of Reform. Caricature by C.F.Grant, 1832. British Museum, London. Photo: Freeman

31 Capital and Labour. Cartoon from Punch, 1843. Photo: Freeman

32 Parish relief. Anon. caricature, 1833. British Museum, London. Photo: Freeman

33 Robespierre. Engraved portrait after Raffet, c. 1847. British Museum, London. Photo: Freeman

34 St-Just. Engraved portrait after Raffet, c. 1847. British Museum, London. Photo: Freeman

35 G. Babeuf. Engraved portrait, c. 1850. Photo: Bulloz

36 A View from the Royal Exchange: Nathan Rothschild. Drawing by R. Dighton, 1817. Photo: Mansell Collection, London

37, 38 Penny of Scotland, 1797. Obverse: Adam Smith; reverse: *Wealth of Nations*. British Museum, London. Photo: Peter Clayton

39 The Road to Ruin. Caricature from *Fun*, 1867. Guildhall Library, London. Photo: Freeman

40 Heading of Robert Owen's periodical *The Crisis*, 1833. British Museum, London. Photo: Freeman

41 St-Simon. Plaster cast of a medal. Bibliothèque de l'Arsenal, Paris. Photo: Foliot

42 The Saint-Simonian community at Ménilmontant. From a publication of 1832. Bibliothèque Nationale, Paris

43 Father Enfantin in the costume of the Order of St Simon. Anon. oil painting. Bibliothèque de l'Arsenal, Paris. Photo: Foliot

44 Berlioz conducting a concert, 1846. Satirical German drawing. Bibliothèque de l'Opéra, Paris.

45 The inauguration of the Suez Canal: passage at El Guisr. Lithograph after a watercolour by E. Riou, 1869, from G. Nicole, *Inauguration du Canal de Suez*, 1869. Photo: Freeman

46 Charles Fourier. Portrait by J. F. Gigoux, 1836. Musée de Besançon. Photo: Michel Meusy by courtesy of Librairie Larousse

47 Plan of a phalanstère after a design by C. Fourier. Signed Victor Considérant. Bibliothèque Nationale, Paris. Photo: Foliot

48 The Lyons uprising: Bataille de la Place des Bernardines, 22 November 1831. Lithograph by Bardoz. Bibliothèque Nationale, Paris. Photo: Bulloz

49 Auguste Blanqui. Portrait drawing by David d'Angers, 1840. Musée Carnavalet, Paris. Photo: Bulloz

50 'Property is Theft.' Caricature of Proudhon from the French satirical journal *Revue Comique*, Paris, 1848. British Museum, London. Photo: Freeman

51 *Le Charenton Ministériel*. Colour lithograph by Honoré Daumier from *La Caricature* No. 83, 1832. British Museum, London

52 The Peterloo massacre, 16 August 1819. Communist Party Library, London. Photo: Brompton Studio

53 Early Trade Union membership card issued to the West of Scotland Power Loom Female Weavers Society, 1833. Photo: Mansell Collection, London

54 Chartist demonstration on Kennington Common, London. Lithograph by Cham (C. D. Noe), 1848. British Museum, London

55 Immanuel Kant. Caricature by Hagemann, 1801. British Museum, London. Photo: Freeman

56 Johann Gottlieb Fichte in the costume of a Berlin Home Guard. Watercolour drawing by C. Zimmermann, 1813. Collection of Hofbaurath A. Schadow, Berlin. Photo: Märkisches Museum, Berlin

57 G. W. F. Hegel. Portrait by J. Schlesinger, Nationalgalerie, Berlin. Photo: Staatliche Museen, Berlin

58 Karl Marx. Caricature after the prohibition of the *Rheinische Zeitung*, 1845. Photo: Brompton Studio

59 The Structure of German Society. Caricature by W. Scholz from the German satirical weekly *Kladderadatsch*, Berlin, 1849. British Museum, London. Photo: Freeman

60 The Coalition. Anon. allegorical cartoon, 1790. Bibliothèque Nationale, Paris. Photo: Foliot

61 *Finis Poloniae*. Painting by D. Mouten, 1830. Nationalgalerie, Berlin. Photo: Staatliche Museen

62 Johann Gottfried Herder. Portrait by J. A. Tischbein, 1796. Photo: Deutsche Fotothek, Dresden

63 *The Bard*. Illustration by J. H. Fuseli to Thomas Gray's poem *The Bard*, 1796. Oskar Rheinhart Foundation, Winterthur

64 The Tsar in peasant's habit unmasks Napoleon as a wolf in sheep's clothing. Russian cartoon by Terebenev, 1814. British Museum, London. Photo: Freeman

65 *The Third of May 1808 at Madrid*. The Shootings on Principe Pío Mountain. Painting by Goya, 1814. Prado, Madrid

66 Alexander I. Engraving by Thomas Wright after a portrait by George Dawe R.A.

67 Metternich. Portrait by Thomas Lawrence, 1818. Windsor Castle. Reproduced by gracious permission of Her Majesty the Queen

68 'The Absentee.' Cartoon on Irish affairs from *The Looking Glass* No. 8, 1830. British Museum, London. Photo: Freeman

69 The Hungarian Academy of Sciences. Engraving by Steinicken after a drawing by H. Lüders, *c.* 1863

70 *Greece Expiring on the Ruins of Missolonghi.* Painting by Eugène Delacroix, 1827. Musée des Beaux-Arts, Bordeaux. Photo: Studio Puytorac, Bordeaux

71 Lord Byron. Portrait from Finden: *Landscape and Portrait Illustrations to the Life and Works of Lord Byron*, 1832. British Museum, London. Photo: Freeman

72 King Otho's entry into Athens. Painting by Peter von Hess, 1832. Bayerische Staatsgemäldesammlungen, Munich

73 The People of Rome. Colour lithograph by J. B. Thomas, from *Un An à Rome*, 1823. British Museum, London. Photo: Freeman

74 *Ritratto Psicografico* of Mazzini; *c.* 1860. British Museum, London. Photo: Freeman

75 Friedrich von Schiller. Portrait by Anton Graff, 1791. Museum für Stadtgeschichte, Dresden. Photo: Deutsche Fotothek, Dresden

76 Goethe in the Campagna. Portrait by Tischbein, 1787. Städelsches Kunstinstitut, Frankfurt

77 Professor H. Steffens' lecture at Breslau, 1813, calling for resistance to Napoleon. Painting by A. Kampf, 1889. Bratislawa University. Photo: Ullstein

78 Baden peasants. Anon. colour lithograph after Tony Johannot, from C. Guinot, *L'Été à Bade*, 1846. British Museum, London. Photo: Freeman

79 Russian folk print, probably first half of nineteenth century. Photo: Freeman

80 Achim von Arnim. Portrait by E. Ströhling, 1804. Photo: Internationes, Bonn

81 Theodore Körner. Portrait by D. Stock, 1813. Nationalgalerie, Berlin. Photo: Staatliche Museen, Berlin

82 E. Moritz Arndt. Portrait by F. Bender, 1843. Nationalgalerie, Berlin

83 Francis I of Austria. Portrait by Thomas Lawrence, 1818. Windsor Castle. Reproduced by gracious permission of Her Majesty the Queen

84 German Customs before the *Zollverein*. Contemporary caricature. Photo: Ullstein

85 The *Zollverein*. Caricature, 1833. Photo: Bildarchiv Lolo Handke

86 *Die Wacht am Rhein*. German caricature, *c.* 1840. Photo: Deutsche Fotothek, Dresden

87 The Bard. Painting by John Martin, 1817. The Laing Art Gallery, Newcastle upon Tyne

88 Jean-Jacques Rousseau. Coloured lithograph from *Vues des différentes habitations de J.J.R.*, 1819. British Museum, London. Photo: Freeman

89 Illustration to Goethe's *Werther* by D. Chodowiecki, Berlin 1775. Photo: Freeman

90 Frontispiece to A. W. Pugin: *An Apology for the Revival of Christian Architecture*, 1843. British Museum, London. Photo: Freeman

91 Frontispiece to Balzac: *Contes Drolatiques*; woodcut by Gustave Doré, 1855. British Museum, London. Photo: Freeman

92 A 'Gothic' garden: view of the chapel in the garden at Strawberry Hill. From Horace Walpole: *A Description of Strawberry Hill*, 1784. British Museum, London. Photo: Freeman

93 Hamlet and his father. Etching by Eugène Delacroix, 1843. Bibliothèque Nationale, Paris

94 Illustration to *Ossian*. Indian ink-wash over pencil drawing by John Sell Cotman, 1803. Courtesy of the Trustees of the British Museum, London

95 Illustration to E. T. A. Hoffmann: *Erzählungen*, 1839 ed. Author's sketch. British Museum, London. Photo: Freeman

96 *Man and Woman gazing at the Moon.* Painting by Caspar David Friedrich, 1819. Nationalgalerie, Berlin

97 Fire at Sea. Painting by J. M. W. Turner, *c.* 1834. Courtesy of the Trustees of the Tate Gallery, London

98 Page from William Blake's *Jerusalem*, 1808-18. Facsimile of the only Illuminated Book, published by the Trianon Press for the William Blake Trust, London. The original is now in the possession of Mr Paul Mellon

99 Stonehenge. Painting by John Constable, 1835. Victoria and Albert Museum, London. Crown copyright

100 Rest on the Flight into Egypt. Painting by Philipp Otto Runge, 1805–6. Kunsthalle, Hamburg

101 Napoleon Crossing the Bridge at Arcola; painting by Antoine Jean Gros, 1796. Louvre, Paris. Photo: Brompton Studio

102 Novalis (Friedrich von Hardenberg); portrait by Eduard Eichens, c. 1845. Akademie der Künste, Berlin

103 Heinrich Heine. Portrait by L.E.Grimm, 1827

104 Adam Mickiewicz. Lithograph after a photograph by Nadar

105 Ludwig van Beethoven. Memorial in Vienna by Zumbusch. Photo: Bildarchiv Lolo Handke

106 The Republic. Painting by Honoré Daumier, 1848. Louvre, Paris

107 Louis Philippe. Caricatures by Charles Philippon. British Museum, London. Photo: Freeman

108 Guizot. Lithograph by Honoré Daumier from La Caricature, 1834. British Museum, London. Photo: Freeman

109 Lamartine addressing a crowd. From the Leipziger Illustrierte Zeitung, 1848. British Museum, London. Photo: Freeman

110 The Barricades. Vignette by G. Courbet for Baudelaire's periodical Le Salut Public, 1848. Bibliothèque Nationale, Paris. Photo: Foliot

111 Paris street urchins in the Tuileries Palace. Lithograph by Honoré Daumier, 1848. British Museum, London. Photo: Freeman

112 An Meine lieben Berliner. Anon. lithograph. Märkisches Museum, Berlin

113 Demagogue in Berlin. From a contemporary pamphlet, 1848. British Museum, London. Photo: Freeman

114 The great barricade in Berlin, 18–19 March 1848. Drawing by J.Kirchhoff from Leipziger Illustrierte Zeitung, 1848. British Museum, London. Photo: Freeman

115 The Frankfurt Assembly in the St Paulskirche. From Leipziger Illustrierte Zeitung, 1848. British Museum, London. Photo: Freeman

116 Deputy at the German National Assembly, Frankfurt. Cartoon by Arnold Schrödter, 1848. Photo: Brompton Studio

117 Metternich fleeing from Vienna at the outbreak of the Revolution. Caricature by Karl Zompis, 1848. Photo: Brompton Studio

118 The publication of the 'Twelve Points' at Pest, 15 March 1848. From Leipziger Illustrierte Zeitung, 1848. British Museum, London. Photo: Freeman

119 Barricade in Milan. From the Leipziger Illustrierte Zeitung, 1848. British Museum, London. Photo: Freeman

120 Neapolitan lazzarone. From the Illustrated London News, 1848. British Museum, London. Photo: Freeman

121 The 'Three Props of the Austro-Croat Civilization': Jelacic, Radetzky and Windischgrätz. From Revue Comique, Paris, 1849. British Museum, London. Photo: Freeman

122 Pope Pius IX. Dutch caricature, 1852. British Museum, London. Photo: Freeman

123 Garibaldi. Engraving by W.Holl after a photograph. After 1848. British Museum, London. Photo: Freeman

124 Count Cavour. Lithograph by E.Desmaisons after a photograph, 1856. British Museum, London. Photo: Freeman

125 Two Utopias. Caricature from Revue Comique, Paris, 1849. British Museum, London. Photo: Freeman

126 Alexander Herzen. Portrait by Nicholas Gay

# INDEX

Africa 15–16
Alexander I of Russia 25, 37, 104, 114, *102*, *105*
Algeria 16, 68
Alsace 179
America 14, 19 (see also: Latin America, United States of America)
Ampère, André-Marie 156
Anarchism 58
Arminius 125, 126
Arndt, Moritz 127, *127*
Arnim, Achim von 127, *127*
Arnim, Count Karl von 177–8
Asia 15
Athens 95
Attwood, Thomas 78, 80
Austerlitz 192
Australia 15
Austria 14, 21, 25, 101, 116, 120, 122, 123, 129, 130ff., 174, 180, 182ff., 186, 187ff., 193
Azeglio, Massimo d' 120

Baal-Shem-Tov 138
Babeuf, François-Noël 52, 57, 78, 82, *53*
Bach, Alexander 187, 189
Baden 30, 181
Bakunin, Michael 163
Balkan peninsula 14, 114
Baltic lands, 98, 134, 138
Balzac, Honoré de 158, *141*
Barbès, Armand 168
Bauer, Bruno 91, 93
Bavaria 30
Bazard, Armand 66
Beethoven, Ludwig van 144, 149, 156, 157, *161*
Belfort 37
Belgium 14, 16, 169
Bentham, Jeremy 47, 56
Berlin 31, 49, 168, 181, *177*
Berlioz, Hector 68, 158, *68*
Berry, Charles, Duc de 37
Bismarck, Otto von 24, 26, 177–8, 182, 189, 191, 192, 193
Blake, William 145, 150, 165, *151*
Blanc, Louis 57, 58, 75, 172
Blanqui, Auguste 24, 57, 73–4, 168, 172, *74*
Bodmer, Jean-Jacques 138
Bohemia 130, 131, 183, 184, 186
Bonald, Louis de 24, 27, 35
Bonhomme (see: Saint-Simon)

Born, Stephan 181
Bourbon, House of 30, 37, 39, 44, 48
Bradford 20
Brandenburg, Count Friedrich Wilhelm von 189
Bray, John Francis 64
Bright, John 80
Britain 9, 15, 37, 76–81, 110, 114, 122, 128, 169, 180, 185 (see also: England)
Bruck, Baron Karl Ludwig von 187
Brussels 82
Bulgarians 113
Bukovina 138
Buonarroti, Philippe-Michel 57
Buret, Eugène 72
Burke, Edmund 27, 28, 124, 150
Burschenschaften 33, 38, *37*
Byron, Lord George Gordon 110, 135, 157, 158, 160, 161, 165, *112*

Cabet, Étienne 75, *195*
Calderon de la Barca, Pedro 142
California 194, *195*
Canada 15, 194
Canning, George 104
Canterbury-Whitstable railway *13*
Cape of Good Hope 15
Carbonari 33, 40
Carignano, Prince de 36
Carlsbad 38
Carlyle, Thomas 68, 163
Carrel, Armand 41
Castlereagh, Henry Robert 104
Cavaignac, General 191
Cavour, Camillo Benso 193, *193*
Cervantes, Miguel de 142
Ceylon 15
Chantelauze, Regis 40
Charles Albert, King of Piedmont and Sardinia 36, 188
Charles X of France 30, 40–1, *41*
Charter (La Charte) 29, 30
Chartist movement, 76–81, *79*
Chateaubriand, François-René de 110, 157
China 15
Cieszkowski, August 93
Cobden, Richard 80
Coburg, Prince Friedrich Josiah von Sachsen-Coburg 96
Coleridge, Samuel Taylor 135, 143, 145, 150, 152–3, 157, 164–5
Colmar 37

Comte, Auguste 63
Condillac, Étienne Bonnot de 152
Condorcet, Antoine-Nicolas de 59
Constable, John 155, *154*
Constant, Benjamin 129, 158
Constantine, Grand Duke of Russia 36
Constantinople 113, 161
Corot, Jean-Baptiste 147
Cortés, Donoso 196
Courbet, Gustave *175*
Cracow 14, 183
Croats 131, 183, 184
Czechs 131, 183, 184, 186

Dante Alighieri 142
Daumier, Honoré 35, *34, 35, 38*, 74, *167*, *175*
David, Jacques-Louis *43*
Decembrist uprising (Russia) 33, 36
Delacroix, Eugène 110, 158, *39*, *110*, *142*
Denmark, 14, 180, 186
De Quincey, Thomas 135
Descartes, René 138, 152
Disraeli, Benjamin (Lord Beaconsfield) 28, 191
Doherty, John 77
Doré, Gustave *29*, *141*
Dresden 30

Egypt 68, 110, 114
Enfantin, Barthélemy-Prosper 66, 67, *67*
Engels, Friedrich 69, 82
England 14, 17, 19, 21, 23, 27, 28, 30, 44, 45, 46, 48, 49, 53, 82, 104, 106, 135, 140, 155, 168 (see also: Britain)
Evangelical movement 29

Faraday, Michael 156
Ferdinand VII of Spain 33
Fête de la Fédération *27*
Feuerbach, Ludwig 24, 90
Fichte, Johann Gottlieb 82, 85–6, 123, 127–8, 153, 157, *87*
Fieschi 74
Filomats and Filarets 33
Fischhof, Dr Adolf 182
Flaubert, Gustave 164
Fourier, Charles 57, 64, 68–71, 75, 82, *70*
France 9, 13, 14, 16, 17, 18, 19, 21, 22, 25, 26, 27, 29–30, 33, 34, 37, 39, 41, 43, 45, 48, 53, 68, 72–75, 76, 80, 81, 82, 94, 95, 102, 103, 114, 117, 123, 124, 128, 135, 140, 141,

157, 166, 168, 169, 170ff., 176, 185, 188, 189ff., 194, *39*, *95*, *167*
Francis I, Emperor of Austria 25, 32, 131, *131*
Francis Joseph, Emperor of Austria 186
Frankfurt Assembly 178ff., 187–8, 192, *179*
Frederick the Great 123
Frederick William III, King of Prussia 25
Frederick William IV, King of Prussia 31, 175, 177, 188, 193, *176*
Freedom of the Press *34, 35*
French Revolution *12, 33*
Friedrich, Caspar David 155, *146*
Froebel, Julius 192
Frontiers, map of European (1815) *15*
Füssli, Johann (Henry Fuseli) 138, *98*

Galicia 130, 138, 183, 185
Galvani, Luigi 156
Garibaldi, Giuseppe 188, 193, *193*
Gentz, Friedrich von 27
Gerlach, Ludwig von 24
Germany 9, 14, 21, 25, 30, 33, 36, 37, 38, 48, 81–94, 96, 98, 101, 102, 103, 106, 108, 109, 118, 121–34, 135, 150, 155, 157, 174ff., 182, 183, 184, 185, 186, 187–8, 192, 193, 194, *126*
Gioberti, Vincenzo 119
Godwin, William 160
Goethe, Johann Wolfgang von 86, 139, 153, 160, 162, *121, 139*
Gogh, Vincent van 163
Goya, Francisco de 162, *163*
Gray, Thomas *99*
Great Elector 126
Greece 14, 16, 63, 106, 110ff., *113*
Gros, Antoine-Jean, Baron *159*
Grout, Donald Jay 144
Grün, Karl 93
Guizot, François 40, 166, 169, 170, *170*

Habsburg, House of 30, 116, 122, 130, 131, 182ff., 186, 187, 188
Hecker, Friedrich 181
Haller, Ludwig von 24, 27
Hamann, Johann Georg 138
Hanover 179
Harney, George Julian 78
Hartley, David 152
Hassidism 38
Hazlitt, William 135
Hegel, Georg Wilhelm Friedrich 12, 82, 86–90, 92, 93, 123, 163, *87*

**213**

Heine, Heinrich 68, 157, 162, *160*
Helmholtz, Hermann von 156
Herder, Johann Gottfried 96ff., 138, *98*
Herschel, Sir John Frederick William 153
Herzen, Alexander 194ff., *196*
Hess, Moses 82, 93
Hodgskin, Thomas 64
Hoffmann, E.T.A. 145, 149, 152, *145*
Hohenzollern, House of 30
Hölderlin, Johann Christian Friedrich 135
Holland 14, 15, 58
Holstein 179 (see also: Schleswig-Holstein)
Homer 142
Hugo, Victor 157, 158
Hume, David 82
Hungary 101, 106, 107, 108–9, 131, 182, 184,
    185, 186, 187, 188, *184*

Iberia 14, 169 (see also: Spain, Portugal)
India 15
Ireland 20, 106
Isabey *16, 42*
Italy 9, 14, 21, 33, 104, 106, 108, 109, 115ff.,
    128, 131, 135, 166, 183, 187, 188, 193

Jahn, F.L., known as Father 127
Japan 15
Jaurès, Jean 163
Jean-Paul 145
Jélačič, General Joseph 186, *187*
Jena 22
Johnson, Samuel 143
July Revolution (1830) *38*

Kant, Immanuel 81, 82–5, 88, 153–4, 176, *83*
Keats, John 135
Kennington 80
Keyser, Eugénie de 146ff.
Kleist, Heinrich von 126, 135
Koenigsberg 49
Körner, Theodor 127, *127*
Kossuth, Louis 184, 186
Kotzebue, August Friedrich Ferdinand 38

Lafayette, General 37, 40, 41
Lamartine, Alphonse de 157, 158, 169, 171–2,
    178, 190, *171*
Lamb, Sir Frederick 9
Lamennais, Félicité de 24, 25, 157
Lassalle, Ferdinand 58
Latin America 106
Latvia 98

Ledru-Rollin, Alexandre Auguste 191
Leipzig 36
Lemberg 183
Leopardi, Giacomo 120
Lesseps, Ferdinard de 68, *69*
List, Friedrich 133
Lithuania 33
Locke, John 53, 54, 152
Lombardy 116, 183
London 82
Louis XVIII, King of France 29, *31*
Louis-Napoléon Bonaparte 189, 190ff.
Louis-Philippe, King of France 166, 169, 170,
    171, *36, 170*
Lovett, William 78
Luddites 37
Luther, Martin 25, 36, 123, 126, 138
Lyons 72, *73*

Macauley, Thomas Babington 46
Macpherson, James 135
Magyars 131, 185, 186
Maistre, Joseph de 24, 25
Malayan peninsula 15
Manchester 20
Manin, Daniele 187
Manteuffel, E. Hans Karl 189
Manzoni, Alessandro 120
Marseilles 112
Marx, Karl 24, 46, 69, 81, 82, 86, 90–4, 118,
    129, 158, 163, 181, 184, 186, 192, *91*
Mayer, Julius Robert von 156
Mazzini, Giuseppe 68, 116, 117ff., 157, 188,
    193, *119*
Mehemet Ali 14, 134
Methodism 29
Metternich, Prince 9, 31–2, 35, 38, 104, 110,
    166, *105, 184*
Mexico 194
Michelet, Jules 68, 163, 169
Mickiewicz, Adam 157, 161, *160*
Mignet, François-Auguste-Marie 40
Milan 183, *185*
Mill, John Stuart 21
Missolonghi 110
Mitteleuropa 174ff.
Modena 33, 183
Moldavia 113
Montalembert, Charles 192
Moravia 130, 183, 186
Mozart, Wolfgang Amadeus 144
Müller, Adam 27, 135

Munich 30
Muraviev, Colonel Apostol Serge 36
Musset, Alfred de 158

Napier, General Sir Charles 80
Naples 33, 108
Napoleon Bonaparte 10, 21, 30, 32, 40, 43,
   44, 48, 88, 101 ff., 123, 127, 136, 157, 158,
   169, *27, 33, 43, 102, 159*
Napoleon III (see: Louis-Napoléon Bona-
   parte)
Natal 16
National, Le 41
Navarino 114
Netherlands 14
Newman, Cardinal John Henry 163
Newport 80
Newton, Isaac 58, 152
New Zealand 15
Nicholas I of Russia 36, 114, 178, 187, 194
Nietzsche, Friedrich 163
Novalis (Friedrich von Hardenberg) 25, 26,
   135, 145, 148, 149, 156, 158, 160, *160*
Novara 187

O'Brien, James Bronterre 78
O'Connor, Feargus 78, 80
Odessa 112
Old Sarum 45
Olmütz 193
Orient 150
Orléans, House of 74, 168, *74*
Orléans, Duc d' 40, 41
Örsted, Hans Christian 156
Ossian 138, 141
Otto of Bavaria *113*
Ottoman Empire 14, 21, 112, 113 (see also:
   Turkey)
Owen, Robert 57, 71, 77, *57*

Palacky, Francicek 186
Panama 58
Pan-Slav Congress 183
Papal State 183
Paris 40, 82, 112, 164, 168, 169, 174, 181,
   191, 194
Parma 183
Paskiewicz, Ivan 186
Pequeur, Constantin 75
Perier, Casimir 40
Pestel, Paul 36
Peterloo 37, 76, *76*

Phidias 110
Piedmont 36, 116, 120, 183, *187*
Pitt, William 96
Pius IX, Pope 188, *189*
Place, Francis 77
Poland 14, 33, 36, 96, 106, 108–9, 131, 135,
   173, 177, 178, 180, 185, 186, 194, *36, 97*
Polignac, Jules-Armand de 41, 44
Poor relief *50*
Portugal 15, 16
Posen 180–1
Prague 183
Proudhon 57, 58, 75, *74*
Prussia 14, 21, 22, 24, 25, 26, 30, 31, 48, 49,
   89, 93, 102, 103, 122, 124, 129, 134, 175,
   178, 180 ff., 187 ff., 193
Pugin *140*

Radetzky, Marshal Joseph-Venceslas 183,
   187, *187*
Radowitz, Prince Johann-Maria von 193
Ranke, Leopold von 163
Raspail, François 190
Reform Bill *45*
Religion, in England *28, 29*; in France *12*;
   Napoleon's re-establishment of *27*
Renan, Ernest 100
Reynolds, Sir Joshua 143
Rhineland 81, 181, *134*
Ricardo, David 53
Richelieu, Armand-Jean du Plessis 134
Riego y Nuñez, Raffaelo, General 36
Riga 96
Ritter, Johann Wilhelm 153, 156
Robespierre, Maximilien 52, 78, 82, *12, 53*
Rochelle, La 37
Rome 25, 95, 100, 115, 116, 119, 174, 188,
   191, 196, *115*
Romieux, Auguste 189, 190
Rothschild, Nathan *54*
Roubaix 20
Rousseau, Jean-Jacques 68, 95, 96, 138, 139,
   *139*
Ruge, Arnold 93
Ruhr 20
Runge, Philipp Otto 155, *155*
Rumanians 112 ff., 131, 183, 184, 185
Russell, Lord John 46
Russia 14, 15, 21, 25, 33, 36, 37, 48, 79, 97,
   101, 102, 112, 115, 129, 135, 173, 177,
   180, 186, 193, 194, 196, *126*
Ruthenians 184

Saint-Etienne 20
Saint-Just, Louis de 52, *53*
Saint-Simon, Claude Henri de 58–65, 82, *63*
Saint-Simonists 65–8, 75, 117, 191
Sand, George 158
Sand, Ludwig 38
Santarosa, General 36
Sardinia 188
Saumur 37
Savigny, Friedrich Karl von 125
Saxony 20, 104, 181
Scandinavia 14
Schelling, Friedrich Wilhelm Joseph 82, 86, 156
Schiller, Friedrich von 121, 153, *120*
Schlegel, A. W. 135, 149
Schlegel, Friedrich 135, 141, 149–50, 153
Schleiermacher, Ernst 158, 160
Schleswig-Holstein 14, 179, 180 (see also: Holstein)
Schmerling, Anton 187
Schopenhauer, Arthur 163
Schwarzenberg, Karl Philipp von 187, 189
Secret Societies 34, 37
Serbs 183, 184
Shakespeare, William 141, 142
Shelley, Percy Bysshe 135, 144, 155, 157, 158, 160
Siberia 15
Sicily 166, 183
Sieyès, abbé Emmanuel-Joseph 95
Silesia 20, 81, 183
Slavs 98, 101, 113, 132, 183, 184, 185, 186, 196
Smith, Adam 47, 54, 133, *54*
Sophocles 110
South Africa 16
Southey, Robert 9–10, 135, 157
Spain 15, 25, 33, 36, 58, 102, 104, 114, 128, *103*
Sparta 95
Staël, Mme Anne-Louise-Germaine de 157
Steffens, Professor Heinrich 125
Stein, Lorenz von 21, 31, 81, 103, 122
Stendhal (Henri Beyle) 158
Stephens, J. R. 78
Stonehenge *154*
Strasbourg 123
Strauss, David-Friedrich 24, 91
Struve, Gustav von 181
Sue, Eugène 191
Suez 68, *69*

Switzerland 169
Széchenyi, Istvan, Count 107

Tacitus 125
Tasso, Torquato 142
Taurogi 102
Teutons 196
Thierry, Augustin 163
Thiers, Adolphe 40, 134, 191
Thomas, Emile 173
Thompson, William 64
Tieck, Ludwig 135
Tischbein *121*
Tocqueville, Alexis Clérel de 46, 168, 173
Tolpuddle 76
Trade unions 77
Transylvania 131
Treitschke, Heinrich von 30
Turgot, Anne-Robert-Jacques 59
Turkey 14, 101, 106, 110, 112, 113–4, 185 (see also: Ottoman Empire)
Turner, J.M.W. 147, 155, *147*
Tuscany 183

Ukrainians 131, 183, 184
United States of America 15, 194

Venice 116, 187
Versailles 79, 122
Vienna 9, 104, 112, 168, 182, 184, *184*
Vienna Congress 16–17, 103, 128, *16*
Vigny, Alfred de 68
Volta, Alessandro 156

Wackenroder, Wilhelm Heinrich 135, 144
Wallachia 113
Wartburg 36, *37*
Warton, Joseph 135, 138
Weitling, Wilhelm 82
Wellington, Arthur Wellesley Duke of 45, 80, 114
Winckelmann, Johann Joachim 139
Windischgrätz, Prince Alfred von 183, *187*
Wordsworth, William 135, 150, 157, 165
Württemberg 30

'Young England' movement 28
Young Hegelians 81, 90
Ypsilanti 112

Zollverein 132–3, *132*, *133*